枯れた
すすきが
まだ美しい
いのちいっぱい
一生けんめいに
生きてきた
からだ
みつを

JAPAN'S MUSIC

Because it has lived life to its fullest,

the dried pampas grass

still looks so beautiful

Mitsuo Aida 相田みつを

Poet and calligrapher

20 May 1924 – 17 December 1991

Produced by Softwood Books, Suffolk, UK

Text © Paul Charlton, 2023

Translation by Aoi Matsushima (松島あおい)

Design by Softwood Books

First Edition

Paperback ISBN: 978-1-3999-7366-3

www.softwoodbooks.com

JAPAN'S MUSIC
日本の音楽

Introduction
はじめに 4

Tokyo - A Beautiful Arrival 12

A First Day in Nagoya 17

Magomechaya Minshuku Guesthouse
民宿　馬籠茶屋...23

Leaving Magomechaya....................................26

To Kyoto from Magome 31

Kyoto - 2022-11-02..34

Tenryu-ji and The Garden of Okochi-Sanso Villa.................38

Ohayōgozaimasu! Good Morning! With Oranges! 44

Seikokuji
清谷寺...50

Marine Line Mishap...58

Red Moon, Monet, and a Red Pomegranate Tree 61

A Huge Cat...68

The Dome
ドーム..72

A Couple on a Tram
路面電車のふたり..78

IN MEMORIAM Hiroshima Prefectural First Girls' High School
追憶　広島県立広島第一高等女学校 85

Enjoying Yamaguchi
山口を楽しむ 94

Across The Generations
世代を超えて 104

Walking in Hagi
萩の散策 109

Six Days in Hagi
萩の6日間 117

Kaneko Misuzu Museum
金子みすゞ記念館 127

Shamisen in Tsuwano 138

Three Girls and Their Umbrellas 144

Inari's Mist 148

The Photo 150

Japan's Music
日本の音楽 154

The Ramen Izakaya
ラーメン居酒屋 165

A Night and A Day in Tokyo 174

The Pit Inn in Shinjuku 178

Arigatōugozaimasu 181

A Japan Postscript
日本　あとがき 185

INTRODUCTION

In March 2023, I wrote to Toshiko Yoshizu. Toshiko san lives in Hagi, a town on the coast of The Sea of Japan and she had shared her and her family's home with me for six days when I travelled in Japan in November 2022. This is my letter.

Toshiko san,

Firstly, I hope you and Naoki san are well and all your family...

I am well and so too are all my family...

I have wanted to send you this card ever since returning from Japan! So, I apologise greatly that I am only doing so now! I want to say, at the same time, that I am still in Japan in my head! The kindness and generosity I received from you and everyone in Hagi shall never leave me ... I want to return tomorrow!!

It is our good fortune that a few times in our lives, wonderful experiences do happen. For me, the month of November which I spent travelling in Japan was one of those rare, wonderful experiences. Staying in your beautiful home and having every moment of every day filled with kindness and happiness was a beautiful gift to my memory.

I travelled to Japan with the unknowingness of an older stranger and returned with a shawl made of beauty which will remain wrapped around me forever ...

I wanted my stories of Japan to come out of my head and so I wrote the poems each day in Japan. Now I want the poems to come out of my computer and onto paper so they are in the light of day!

When they are done, and we have a book of poetry, you will have a copy!

もう一度どうもありがとう*

Take care,

Paul Charlton

*もう一度どうもありがとう is pronounced *mōichido dōmo arigatō* and means *Thank you very much again.*

This collection of poems is an account of my travel through Japan's central island, Honshu, with a backpack at age 70. My teacher of Japanese, Lisa Omura, suggested that I describe the circumstances of each poem as to when, where, how I wrote it, how I felt, what happened on the day, who's point of view it was from, and its connections with other events.

This was a really good idea, as it allowed me to better remember the flow and the intricacies of these wonderful experiences. Hopefully, it also helps by making the poems more concrete when reading them.

The title, *Japan's Music,* is taken from the poem in the book.

These poems are about the extraordinary wonder that rarely inhabits our lives but which, when it does, leaves us at our most happy.

Some of the poems are accompanied by a translation into Japanese. These translations are as a thank you to the individuals who made those poems happen.

はじめに

　2023年3月に、ヨシズ・トシコさんに手紙を書きました。トシコさんは萩という日本海沿いの街にご家族とお住まいで、私は2022年11月に日本を訪れた際、6日間泊めていただきました。これが私の手紙です。

　トシコさんへ

　トシコさん、ナオキさん、そしてご家族の皆様、お元気でしょうか。

　わたしも家族も元気です。

　私は日本から英国に帰国して以来ずっと、このカードをお送りしたいと思っていました！　それなのに今になってしまい、本当に申し訳ありません。でも、まだ私は頭の中では日本にいるのです！ 萩のトシコさんや皆さんの優しさと惜しみないご親切を忘れたことはありません。明日にも萩に戻りたいです。

　幸運なことに、人生には何度か素晴らしいことが起きます。わたしにとって、日本を旅した11月は、その貴重な、素晴らしい体験のひとつでした。トシコさんのすてきな家に泊めていただき、優しさと幸せに包まれて過ごした日々のすべては、美しい思い出となりました。

　私は日本に着いた時には何も知らない年配のよそ者でしたが、帰国する時には美しい思い出で紡がれたショールをまとっており、それはこれからも永遠に私を包んでくれるでしょう……

　私の日本での経験を表現したくて、滞在中に毎日詩を書きました。その詩を、今度はコンピューターから印刷し、日の目を見せようと思います。

　詩集が完成したら、お送りします。

　もう一度どうもありがとう

　お元気で。

　ポール・チャールトン

この詩集は、私が70歳の時にバックパックを背負って、日本の本州を旅した記録です。そして私の日本語教師のオオムラ　・リサ先生が、それぞれの詩をいつ、どこでどのように書いたのか、どう感じたか、その日に何があったか、誰の視点で書いているか、その他の出来事との関連などを書くことを勧めてくれました。

この良いアイディアのおかげで、様々な素晴らしい体験の流れや結びつきを、より良く記憶することができました。願わくば、それによって詩を読んだ時に、より具体的に感じられればと思います。

『日本の音楽』という題名は、収録された詩のひとつからとりました。

この一連の詩は、最高に幸せな気持ちをもたらしてくれる、人生でも稀にしか起こらない素晴らしい体験について書いています。

いくつかの詩には、日本語の翻訳をつけました。この翻訳に、この詩が生まれるきっかけを作ってくださった方々への感謝を込めました。

TOKYO

2022-10-28
A Beautiful Arrival

On my first morning in Japan, I met my Japanese teacher Lisa Omura – Lisa sensei. Japanese peoples' names are accompanied by a title, or honorific, such as *san,* a gender-neutral word for Ms, Mrs, and Mr. Sensei is the word for teacher.

I met Lisa sensei in a hotel in Tokyo ... it was amazing!

She catapulted me into a state of mind that I remained in for every single day that I was in Japan! When I left Lisa sensei that evening my mind, my heart, and my body had been taken to a place of tranquillity – of calmness and peace. My senses – eyes, nose, ears, touch, and taste – had been opened to Japan and its people and places and everything that was there to come in the next four weeks ...

Lisa sensei gave me gifts in a manner that I had never experienced before. Her smile of welcome when she called my name in the reception area, the feeling of total surprise and unknowing about anything, of being led to the hotel's little lounge, the welcome of the gifts that she poured onto the table, with every single moment of that day, I was given the purest of hearts and minds with which to travel in Japan. I stayed like that for the next 30 days and a good part of me still is there!

It was the most beautiful of arrivals.

I travelled from Tokyo to Nagoya on the extraordinary bullet train – *the shinkansen.*

I wanted to write down what had happened that day and how I felt that evening. In the hotel room in Nagoya, I started to write like a diary but instead a first poem happened. This poem was not planned ... it was the only way I could tell the story of the most beautiful of arrivals.

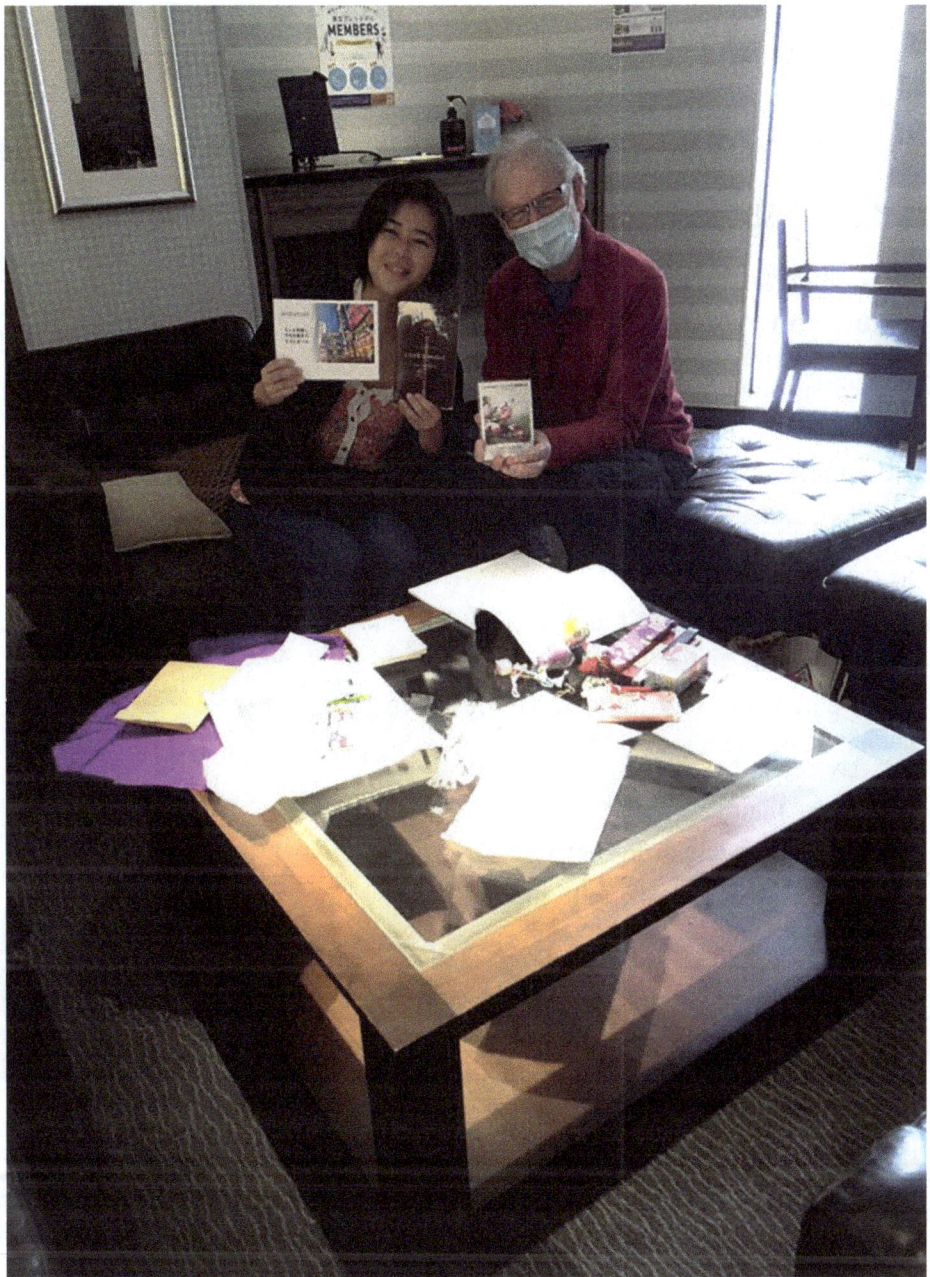

A BEAUTIFUL ARRIVAL

'sensei' is the word for 'teacher' in Japanese.
'ekiben' means 'the station shop'.

'どうもありがとうございます'

'**Dōmo arigatōugozaimas**' is how this phrase is pronounced.
'**Thank you very much**' is its meaning.

Lisa sensei said
The Tokyo Imperial Palace
Is the main residence of the Emperor of Japan.
Bags left in a station locker; we went there.

Lisa sensei said
Warriors once fired their arrows at us
Defending the castle from our attack.
Now we just turn left and admire the stone.

The day actually started in a hotel lobby,
"I thought I would give you a surprise!"
Was the most beautiful greeting.
Lisa sensei said.

I sat in the lounge surrounded by her gifts
One by one opening the whole of Japan
A fan, soft owls, drawings on a card, much more
Lisa sensei said.

The date matters, 2022-10-28
A day a hot sun pretended it wasn't autumn
Except it was, on the grass in Tokyo
Lisa sensei said.

The Imperial Palace had decided not to play
The leaves on the trees, the flowers on the street
The open spaces standing guard, will do instead,
Lisa sensei said.

And what about Shinkansen, luggage lockers for bright backpacks,
An *ekiben* store for red bean rice cakes and sushi on the train,
Reserving a ticket to depart, the 15.33 to Nagoya
Lisa sensei said.

A beautiful arrival.

どうもありがとうございます
Dōmo arigatōugozaimas

Paul san said.

NAGOYA

2022-10-29

I woke up and went downstairs to the hotel's self-service breakfast. I was full of curiosity. I was full of energy. I welcomed the Japanese food – the Asian breakfast!

My plan was simple for this first day on my own. It was to relax and to become familiar with being in Japan – nothing to panic or overwhelm. My plan was to have a day in a city where I could easily get around and do simple tourist things.

I looked at the tourist guide for Nagoya and chose a Japanese garden and a Japanese castle. I worked out that it was sensible to firstly go to the Shirotori Garden. I went by train as I was not confident yet to use a bus.

The hotel was ten minutes' walk to the train station. I walked there slowly, absorbing the visual – noticing clothes, the ages of people, the Japanese language signs. I absorbed the sounds, not just the language. The streets were youthful.

At the station, I could not work out which train and which platform and how to buy a ticket. There were many different train lines, and the English signage was not detailed enough. So, I walked backwards and forwards from one part of the station to another, as I was interested in what was happening around me and as to where I was heading.

After 30 minutes or so ... (I wasn't bothered, I was patient), I saw a small, one-person, information kiosk saying, 'English Spoken'. Ahh! There was a young woman – her English was good enough to tell me which platform and how to get there. And she was so friendly!

So, on the train I went ... looking, looking, listening, listening! It seemed like quite a long time on the train, including carefully changing stations. I walked at least 40 minutes, still slowly, from the station to the Garden. I saw my first Buddhist temple, plain and tucked away in a side street, and stood there for a while.

I walked into Shirotori Garden and stood, immediately stunned by its beauty ... a traditional Japanese garden – the size of a park. It was like arriving in a dream!

There was an explanation in English of the garden design. It was laid out according to the nature and geography of the region. The nearest part to me was of a mountain river ... I walked on a path made of large stones. I sat by the little river for a long time just listening to its flowing sound.

Then I walked through a small bamboo forest ... I saw a bride and groom in traditional dress with the photographer on a bridge. Everywhere my eyes arrived in this Japanese garden was upon a beauty I had never experienced before.

Then Nagoya Castle ... I walked there. A traditional Japanese castle ... again it was like arriving in a dream! As I walked through the main gate, a woman approached and spoke to me in English. Smiling, she offered to guide me at no cost. I was very happy to accept. Her name, Yaeda, I hope I shall never forget! She gave me all the information which is in the poem.

After Nagoya Castle, I caught another train and arrived back at Nagoya station. I only then realised how huge it is as I tried to find my way out. It was just outside the station that I saw this astonishing and amusing huge mannequin, Nana Chan, I looked up more information about her for the poem.

I didn't eat that day until the evening. On the way back to the small hotel I saw the restaurant, Kikuya, in a side street. It had an open window so I could see in! It was a modern and open design, so a safe place for me to try my first Japanese meal in a restaurant!

I had no idea what I was ordering! But it did not matter, I knew I would eat whatever I was given ... and I loved it!

A First Day in Nagoya

A first day in Nagoya,
Working out how to board a local train.
Found an information booth, only one woman
With a smile and just enough English.

The intention to make my way to the Shirotori Garden.
Breathtaking!
Designed according to a map of the region's geography,
I walked past rivers and through a bamboo forest
Leaves still green, not quite changed to autumn.
A bride on a bridge, traditionally dressed
The groom similarly so, standing to her side.

Then to the magnificent castle and palace,
Side by side and rebuilt after their World War II destruction,
Their restoration rich with materials recreating their past.
The scented palace, made entirely of cypress wood,
Its form identical to the original,
Made from trees, 600 years old,
Harvested and brought from distant mountains.

Those possessions of a 17th century Tokugawa shogun.
Golden sea creatures with tiger-like heads adorning the top
The motif throughout a hollyhock,
Asserting allegiance to the castle lord.
Opposing the Emperor's own, the chrysanthemum.

And a guide whose name, Yaeko,
Means a five-petalled flower!
She explained the division of the palace rooms
Each accorded a status according to the rank of the visitor.
The more elaborate the room and its paintings,
The more elevated the guest, the nearer to the shogun.

It was dark coming off the train on the way back
The more stunning the gigantic mannequin outside the station.
At the Meitetsu Department Store is Nana-chan.
She stands 20-feet tall with a thin, long neck, long legs.
Her costume that day a blue dress and a rainbow mask.

The evening restaurant 'Kikuya', meaning chrysanthemum.
'Soba and food, delicious sake', the menu said.
Chilled noodles, a beautiful bowl,
Rice, steamed and locally flavoured,
Its bowl too, perfect on the bamboo tray.
Sake, glass ice filled, at the end of the meal!

I sat in a corner, had everyone dining ahead.
The kitchen was mostly open
One waitress moving backwards and forwards,
Background jazz played above my head.
A pine layered, very modern décor
Compartmentalised traditional style,
Giant blue and red flowers
Opened out on the back wall.
Not so romantic, more friends for relaxed dining,
Than for love and marriage intentions.

A first night out in Japan.
For me, it was perfect!

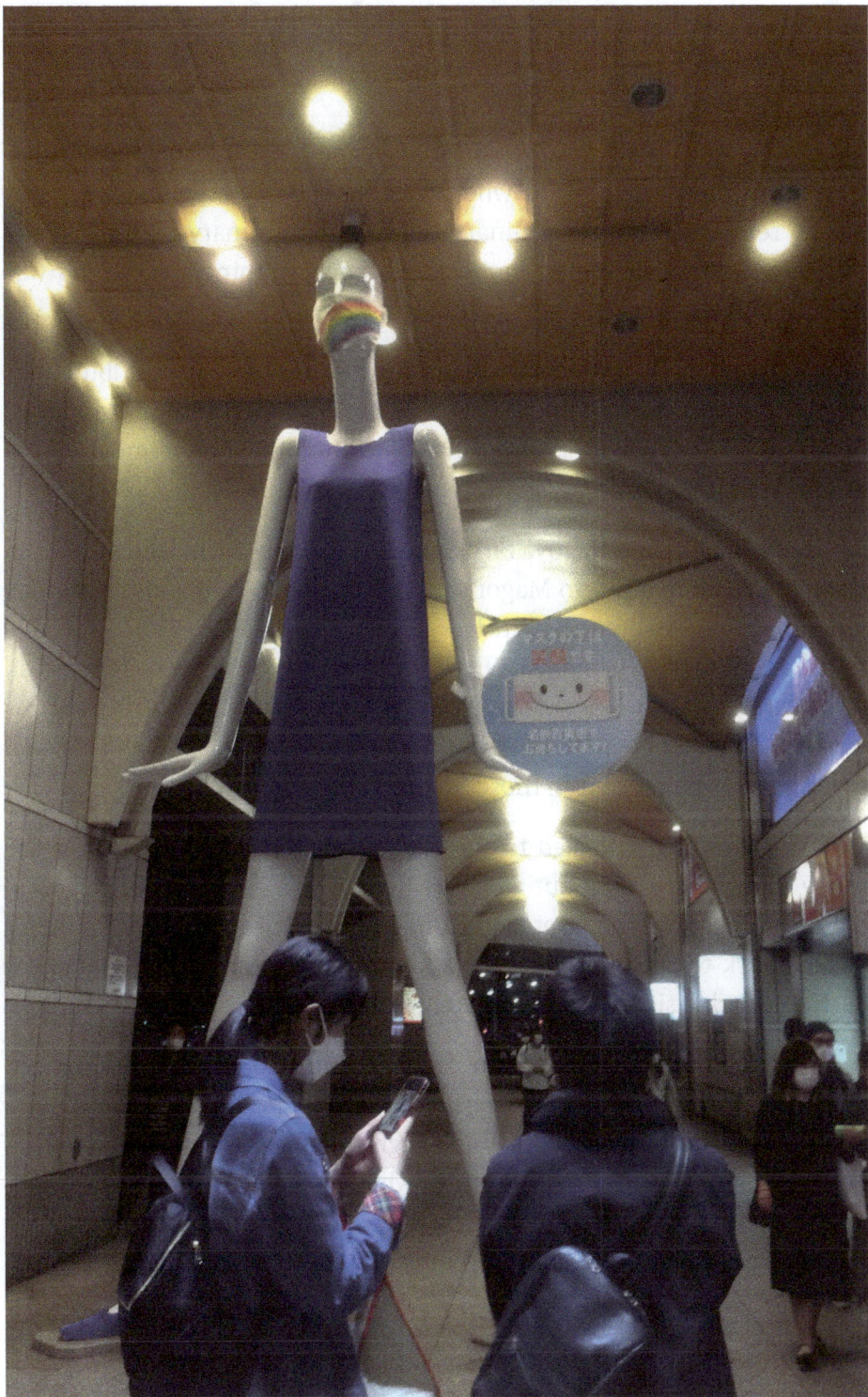

MAGOMECHAYA MINSHUKU GUESTHOUSE

This poem speaks of my extraordinary experience in Magome, in the traditional guest house and when walking the Nakasendo Way. I was totally removed from my ordinary self and my ordinary places. I really was in a state of delighted innocence. I knew nothing, everything was new, and all was of the most extraordinary beauty.

Magome is a protected village – with its Edo period buildings climbing a very steep street. This was my first step into a traditional Japanese guest house, a ryokan. Inside, I felt completely removed from anything that was ordinary in my usual life in the UK.

I took a bus from Nagoya on a Sunday. I had to walk maybe 3 km from the main road up a hill to Magome. I arrived about 3pm and the Sunday Japanese tourists were still quite busy. But I liked that – it was comfortable to have the feel of a Sunday day out. I was carrying my backpack, so had to be careful of other people walking up from the bottom of the narrow and very steep stone path through the town. I was entranced and allowed myself just to be present in those first moments.

That evening, I walked to the top of the town and looked over the range of hills spreading out as far as I could see. A sunset lit the world orange and yellow and stretched from one end of the sky to the other. I walked back to the guest house, to my room with its calming Japanese aesthetic and design. I felt completely at ease.

My poem is not enough to describe the two days and nights in Magome. The walk to the next post town along the Nakasendo Way was 8 km. It was through the forest and high hills, past shrines, and with a beautiful old man offering free tea in what seemed like an ancient barn. His hospitality was utterly wonderful. I wrote the poem that evening, in a dream like state, in the beautiful room after eating beautiful *kaiseki* food.

Kaiseki is a meal with its dishes brought to the table all at the same time and made with local and seasonal ingredients.

I had sat by myself at a table with my food and with my cup of tea filled many times. Earlier, after the walk, I had gone into a gift shop and spoken a little Japanese.

民宿　馬籠茶屋

　この詩は、馬籠の伝統的な宿に泊まり、中山道を歩いた、私の素晴らしい経験を描いています。普段の自分自身や住み慣れた場所とは全く異なる経験でした。まさに無邪気な喜びの境地でした。何も知らず、すべてが新しく、類い稀なく美しかったのです。

　馬籠は昔ながらの町並みが保存されている所で、江戸時代の建物が坂道に並んでいます。これが私の日本の伝統的な民宿初体験でした。中に入ると、イギリスでの普段の生活とは何もかもかけ離れていました。

　私は日曜日に名古屋からバスに乗りました。馬籠までは、降車後3キロほど坂道をのぼりました。到着したのは午後3時頃で、まだ週末の観光を楽しむ日本人で賑わっていました。日曜日のお出かけ気分で、嬉しくなりました。バックパックを背負っていたので、他の人にぶつからないよう注意しながら、街を抜ける狭くて急な石畳の道をのぼって行きました。その瞬間をうっとりと味わいながら。

　その夕方、街の頂上まで行き、見渡す限りに連なる山並みを眺めました。端から端まで広がる空を、夕日がオレンジ色や黄色に染めていました。宿に戻ると、落ち着いた日本美が感じられる部屋で、とてもくつろぎました。

　私の詩では、馬籠での2泊の旅を書き尽くしていません。中山道の次の宿場までは8キロの道のりでした。森と高い丘を越えて、神社を通り、おそらく古い納屋と思われる場所で出会った品のある老人が、お茶をご馳走してくれました。心のこもったもてなしでした。その夕方、私は美しい部屋で美味しい日本料理を食べた後、夢見心地で詩を書きました。

　夕食では、地元産の季節の食材を使った料理が、すべて一緒に運ばれてきました。

　私はひとり食卓につき、何度もお茶をお代わりしました。その前に、散歩から戻った時、土産物屋で少し日本語で話しました。

Magomechaya Minshuku Guesthouse
2022-10-30

In a guest house in Magome
In a six-tatami matted room,
I laid down on my futon
And stopped for a two-night stay
On the old Edo to Kyoto, Nakasendo Way.

The bedcover had a traditional design,
Pale yellow, green leaves and muted
Red flowers.
The table alongside was two hands tall
Enough, with a cushion, for a writer to write on.

No ornaments or designs interrupted the walls,
A single light green colour, gracing
The wide planked wooden ceiling.
A wardrobe's whole wall sliding doors,
Inviting its deep recesses for storage.

A black and white yukata lay there,
A robe to wear when refreshed
By a shower or a bath, after a day's long walk.
Its gold threaded belt perfectly folded,
Crossed and knotted and left upon the top.

The other guests' voices could be heard
Downstairs and along the corridor.
But it's not late and there are notices
Saying sound travels easily
In a building built some 400 years ago.

Hiroshige's print, Miyanoshi-juku
Sits above the door to my room.
The name, one of sixty-nine post towns
With guest houses like this one
Meeting travellers on the Nakasendo Way.

Dinners ... well ... they were exquisite kaiseki.
The tastes still held of whole fish and sashimi,
Tempura and tofu with warm Japanese tea,
A small cauldron of mixed mushrooms.
Beautiful bowls honouring my hands.

民宿　馬籠茶屋
2022年10月30日

馬籠の宿
6畳の部屋に
布団を敷き
2晩を過ごす
江戸から京都を結ぶ中山道の途中

掛け布団の伝統的な柄
淡い黄色と緑の葉
渋い赤色の花
手のひら二つ分の高さの卓
座布団があれば、物書きには十分

壁には無駄な装飾はなく
優美に薄緑一色
幅広の板張りの天井
壁一面の引き戸は
奥行きの深い押入れ

置いてある黒と白の浴衣は
一日の長い散策の疲れを洗い流した
風呂上りの後にまとう衣
金糸の縫い目の帯がきれいに畳んで
結ばれ、浴衣の上に置かれている

他の客の声が
下の階や廊下から聞こえてくる
まだ遅くはなく、注意書きもある
音がよく伝わるのは
400年前の建物だから

広重の版画『宮ノ越宿』が
部屋の入口の上にかかっている
六十九次の宿場のひとつ
ここと同じような宿が
中山道の旅人を迎えたことだろう

夕食は……なんとも見事な日本料理
忘れられぬ味、丸ごとの魚や刺身
天ぷらや豆腐、温かい日本茶
さまざまなキノコの小鍋

LEAVING MAGOMECHAYA

A Haiku

2022-11-01

Leaving Magomechaya
Memories forever made
Autumn's colours wave.

I wrote this short poem on the bus after leaving Magome and the Magomechaya guest house. I wrote it as a desire to connect to the haiku tradition.

This is because I had stood for a long time at the very beautiful memorial stone and garden to the great haiku poet, Basho, near the guest house. I knew I wanted to connect my memory to the Basho stone and garden.

So, a haiku!

I was in awe of where I was – I could not believe I was walking along an ancient path next to this memorial on a hillside in Japan!

It was an autumn day with warmth and also rain.

I had wanted to try and write a poem with a Japanese rule! As respect to where I had been.

A poem of Basho's is written on the stone.

It refers to Autumn – so I had wanted to do the same.

This is Basho's poem on the memorial stone, referring to Kiso, a village not far from Magome in the central alps.

送られつ送りつ果ては木曽の穐

Okuraretsu / okuritsu hate wa / Kiso no aki

After being seen off

And seeing off

The Kiso autumn.

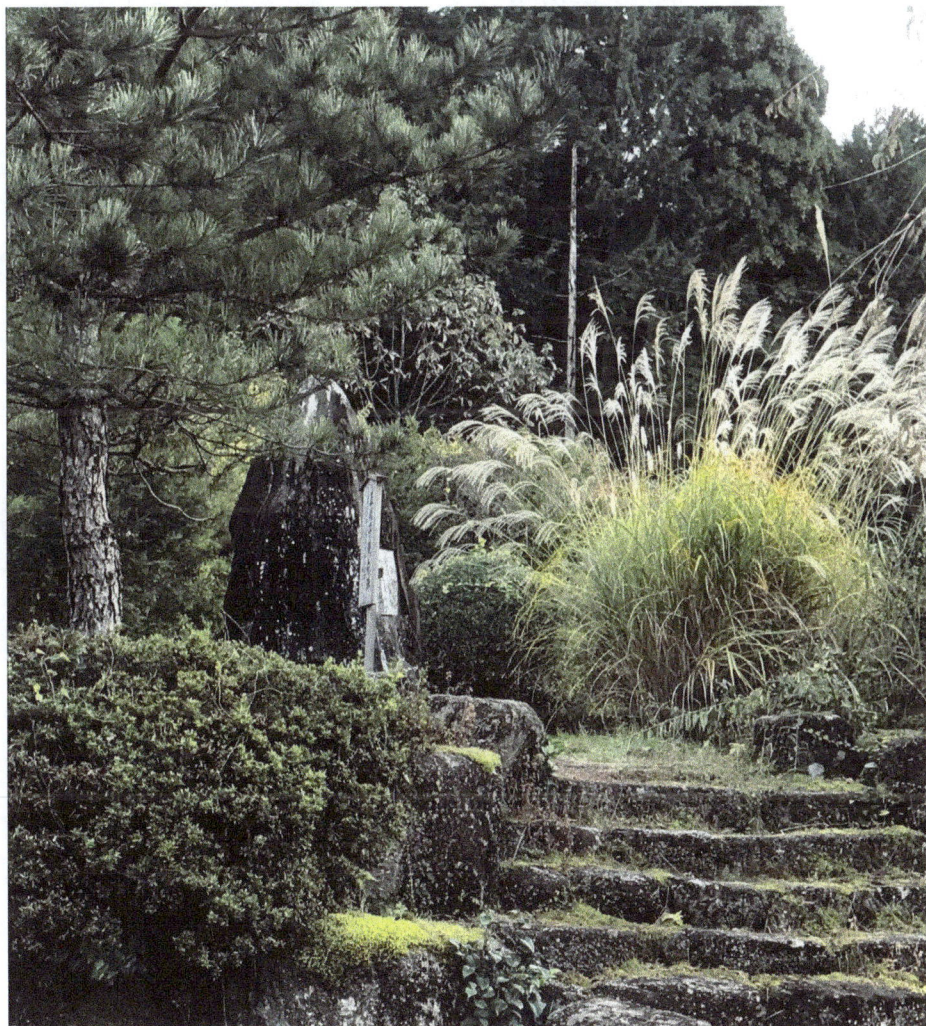

TO KYOTO FROM MAGOME

2022-11-01

I wrote this poem in my room on my first night in Kyoto.
I had travelled from Magome by bus to Nagatsugawa.
The bus was very small.
The journey was down from the high hills of Magome.
So, it was a wandering journey through small villages and around and down the steep hills!
It went past the Basho memorial.

     I loved this bus journey!
This was because I was given views of Japan through the window of the bus.
I was still only in Japan a few days and my eyes, ears, and nose were wide open with amazement.
I saw my first rice field in Magome! The bus drove past them.

     I then travelled by train from Nagatsugawa to Kyoto.
I loved the sound of the name 'Nagatsugawa'!
I knew I wanted to write a poem with this name in it!

     This poem has verses of four lines each.
The shape of my poems come intuitively.
The first thoughts that come into my head have a length.
This length I do not know until the thought is finished!
The first verse, therefore, explains simply that this is a journey from Magome to Kyoto.

     I use the word 'comfortable' many times in the poem.
The feeling I had was of being so at ease, of being welcome.
No anxiety, no fear – only a feeling of comfort all through the day and evening.
It is important to keep this feeling of being comfortable in any translation.

The poem is a first thank you to the Japanese people who gave me this welcome and comfort.

It also says, "I respect you." This why I say the bus 'politely descended'.

The store in Kyoto where I bought the shoes was a large department store opposite the station.

I felt brave when I went in!

I carefully found the shoes I wanted. The young woman was so good-humoured!

I think I amused her and her colleague. We smiled a lot as we succeeded in communicating.

I felt I had been given a precious gift – not the shoes, but the beautiful and comfortable encounter.

The sushi restaurant had a father and a son as chefs. The son spoke a little English.

There were three other people, two women and a man enjoying themselves.

They also welcomed me with amused and friendly curiosity – so I was made comfortable.

They connected me to their evening – like them, I was ok to be in a sushi restaurant in Kyoto.

After buying the shoes, I went back to Kyoto station to catch the underground.

Again, I really liked the sound of the name 'Marutamachi'!

In the station I walked around and discovered it is a huge marketplace!

Again, I loved that – all that Japanese!

And I was more confident – so I asked how to ask for 'sugar'!

It is *sato o kudasai* – could I have sugar, please?

To Kyoto from Magome

It rained today, but politely.
A little wet,
Comfortable on a bus and then a train.
To Kyoto from Magome.

I needed to buy
More comfortable trainers.
Walked, yes wet, into a store.
Left, wearing new soft blue ones.

My spoken Japanese
Comes more comfortably to my head.
There's only one rule,
To be just so polite in everything that's said.

Like asking in the café
For the Japanese for 'sugar'.
Instead of stumbling with "suka"
I can now comfortably say *sato o kudasai*.

I hadn't imagined this magic
Because that's what it is.
Not one moment not comfortable,
Leaving Magome for a train at Nagatsugawa,

The local bus left the highway
And politely descended perpendicularly
Past the memorial to Basho!
I bowed, left a haiku as a memory.

Took a subway to the new accommodation
A small offbeat hotel near Marutamachi station.
A guide, Yoko, is booked for tomorrow,
To view Kyoto's "hidden gems", the persuasive offer.

In a family run small sushi space,
Intimate and comfortable,
A man and two women sat just a few feet away.
Creating a carefree and connecting conversation.

The menu's offer was of three glasses of sake
For those like me, not Japanese
To taste the regional flavours.
I preferred the Shuhari, the sake from Kyoto.

KYOTO

2022-11-02

I wrote this poem in the evening after my first full day in Kyoto. I had it arranged for a guide. This turned out to be a brilliant idea. She met me at a local train station, beside a small supermarket. She took me to a wonderful ice cream shop. She also took me to a pottery, where I bought bowls as gifts for my children.

But above all, she took me to the temples and their gardens. She explained the etiquette of going in and of being inside them. There were not many people, I was lucky.

Lisa sensei had given me the card with Mitsuo Aida's beautiful expression of love.
His words expressed how I felt about this one day in Kyoto. I felt it was possible to use his words about a place and not only a person.

This poem is intended to express the sense of a prayer. A prayer of respect to the temples and shrines, themselves places of prayer.
This poem is also a prayer to the nature of beauty, as seen and experienced by me that day.

The beauty is not only of place but is also of the people.
The young woman inside the post office,
The guide and musician and singer, Yoko.

The design is of a chant ... like a Buddhist chant,
Provoking reflection and meditation and giving thanks.

I felt humble when I wrote this poem.

"あなたの顔を　みていると　こころの中の　波がしずまる"

"As I look upon your face, the waves of trouble in my heart calm down."
Mitsuo Aida

Kyoto - 2022-11-02

Tōfuku-ji is a Buddhist temple in Higashiyama-ku, an area of Kyoto.

One of the best conversations
I have ever had happened
Today,
At four temples in Higashiyama-Ku,
Kyoto,
Japan.

Really, it is two conversations.
Today,
In the Kyoto Central Post Office,
There was another one.
Understanding the world, by posting a parcel
By means of many smiles
And an utterly untroubled patience.

Yoko,
My guide,
Had shown me
Temples,

Tōfuku-ji,
Buddha
Softening minds.
Shinto's
Vermillion Bridges,
Torii gates.
Trees,
Leaves,
Becoming red.
Stones
In ponds,
As demons
After centuries
Now being restored.
Water dropping,
Resonating,
My ear heard a harp.
Six beautifully made ceramic cups.
Red bead bracelet.
Steps over thresholds
Shoes untied.
Chrysanthemums,
Protecting the Emperor.
The Mitera Sennyuji Temple,
An exhibition within, Mikei,
"An approach to things yet to be seen".
Dragons painted on ceilings.
Gardens,
Windows,
Calligraphy,
Contemplation.
Offering
Candles
Connecting
Lovers,

Parents
Now gone.
Incense
Purifying
Renewing the air.

All these words
Make a mantra.
Sumi masen,
I bow to be forgiven
By those places also seen,
but not in this poem.

Each word,
Has the most beautiful image,
I can touch tonight,
Tomorrow becoming forgotten.
What I have been given,
By those Buddhas
In their temples,
Mitsuo Aida has already said,

"As I look upon your face,
the waves of trouble in my heart calm down."

КЧОТО

Tenryu-ji and The Garden of Okochi-Sanso Villa

This day was the first day I left my room in the morning knowing that at the end of the day, I would write a poem. I was therefore now more observant, more attentive to the detail of what I was seeing and hearing.

This poem then is the first poem when I knew I was also perhaps writing for someone else to read.

On this morning, I sat and ate breakfast in a beautiful baker shop and restaurant near where I was staying. I had bought a roll there the previous day and they recognised me. The welcome was beautiful.

I use the word 'beautiful' again and again ... it is the right word. 'Beautiful' is normally a word to use occasionally – but my every day in Japan was filled with beauty ... so 'beautiful' is what happened and is the right word.

An advantage of being within a tourist path busy with other people also intent on seeking to know and to try and understand what is being visited, is that sometimes you are observing them too. This poem begins with the presence of a beautiful infant, newly walking, and feeling her way into her world by picking up stones.

The beauty of the Tenryu-ji temple, its landscape and its bird, a crane in an autumn's deep blue sky, was her backdrop. All eliding into perfection.

And then I walked into the gardens of the Okochi-Sanso villa, once the estate of the film actor Okochi Denjiro (1898–1962).

At the end of this poem is the WhatsApp message I sent to my family about these days.

The message was sent at the time and reveals my joy in the face of the beauty I was experiencing in Kyoto's temples and gardens.

Kyoto
Tenryu-ji and The Garden of Okochi-Sanso Villa

An infant girl played with hand sized stones.
She picked them up one a time,
Teetering, as she tossed them aside.
Each movement determined, designed.

Her father was standing
An arm's reach away
Yet, not really nurturing
Impatient for the mother returning.

In front of her,
An exquisitely crafted pond
Held a crane sat perched on a stone.
An artist's ink in white and grey.

Hills coloured green, amber, orange, and red
Confirmed everything the guidebooks said.
Adorning the crane, again incredibly,
Was a pure blue sky, still burning in November.

Behind the girl
The temple of Tenryu-ji.
All three, crane – girl – temple – in one connected line,
Unbelievable to see.

Within Tenryu-ji,
A dragon coiled its wisdom
Around wall after wall.
I drew closer, being outside
And the unmistakeable scent from lilies
Drew my senses momentarily.

No doubt ikebana, it had to be so,
A tall and very precious looking vase
Gathered an assembly of flowers
Cornered, in the temple's main hall.

I could have stopped then and gone home.

After all, I had had ...

A Kyoto autumn's changing leaves
A November pure blue blazing sky
An evolving infant girl,
A real crane, though preciously ornamental,
And a world heritage temple,
Tenryu-ji.

But – not a word yet said as to
The Garden of Okochi-Sanso Villa,
A few metres only from the temple exit.
Kyoto's distant hills a background landscape
The composition called shakkei, "borrowed scenery."

I had sat transfixed by its beauty
By the calm of its aesthetic,
An open tearoom bordered by bamboo,
A first matcha tea.

How to find the words yet again
As truly the moment does not transcend.

Fortunately, at the time,
I had sent my family a photo and a text.

It said,

Morning 🧡 xxx my incredible good fortune continues in Kyoto 🍁 right now it's 23C, and this view I've taken as I write this text is from a stone seat in one of Kyoto's national treasure gardens 🍁 Kyoto's temples and gardens in autumn are incredible and magnificent … there's no moment I would have left out … like a 9pm salad from the 7/11 last night! The guide yesterday took me to temples and shrines … exposing and involving me in the temple intents … lighting candles and incense sticks in more hidden places away from the grounds … the imperial family's private temples and gardens it turns out today I've gone with the crowds which is also gr8 … seeing the hired kimonos and the families with grandparents and grandkids … I'm walking round one of Kyoto's most famous temples and gardens … indescribably beautiful xxx

KYOTO

2022-11-05

Ohayōgozaimasu! Good Morning! With Oranges!

I had my last breakfast at the beautiful French style baker and restaurant.
The very friendly member of staff gave me the loyalty card.
She stamped it for when I next come back!
I still have the loyalty card in my wallet.
I then took a train to Kyoto station.

After I put my bag in the locker, I took a photo of the number!
I then looked in my little book guide to Kyoto.
I had bought the little book in Kyoto station when I first arrived.
The poem explains that I chose to visit Sanjusangendo Temple because of its 1001 golden statues.

I decided to walk to the temple because the buses were packed!
I like walking as I can feel where I am.
But I got muddled with my satnav!
Because of this, I arrived in a street with a sensory design.
The pavement was created with different textures.
This meant that when walking here, people had different sensations through their feet.
It was called a reflexology space!
Unusual and amusing.

A young couple with a child in a pram were walking in front of me.
They were very together – obviously in love.
I remained behind them to enjoy the connection to their love.
We crossed over the river, and they went in a different direction.

I was then standing at the bottom of a steep hill –
The temple direction was up this hill.
I saw the little shop with fruit and vegetables outside.
The poem describes what then happened.

I felt so happily connected to the old woman and her *Ohayogozaimasu*! The simple beauty of the encounter felt physical ... I felt no separation between us ... she just welcomed me with joy and gave me my oranges.

It was as if I was a customer – a neighbour – who came to her shop every day! I felt so at ease! I knew I wanted to keep this memory alive, so I walked back in front of the shop and took the photo.

The poem does not say anything about being at the temple.

This is because I was completely astounded by the magnificence and power of the 1001 gilt statues – Bodhisattvas – goddesses of compassion.

I wanted the reader of the poem, if possible, to have a sense of this. The last line is meant to give that impression. Nothing else about the temple mattered.

When I returned to Kyoto station, I could not find my locker!

I looked and looked! At last, I found an information kiosk.

The very helpful woman there said my locker was on the other side of the station! I found the locker with only four or five minutes to catch my train. This is when I hurt my back a little, rushing to lift my bag on my back.

I ran to the platform – there was only one minute left!

おはようございます! is spoken as Ohayōgozaimasu! and means Good Morning!

Ohayōgozaimasu! Good Morning! With Oranges!

Arigatōgozaimashita in the poem means thank you.

Ohayōgozaimasu! Good Morning! With Oranges!

I was on my way to the temple, Sanjusangendo,
established I was to learn, in 1164.
I was glad, four perfect days in a row,
And now, with love in my heart,
I was leaving Kyoto.

I had had breakfast in the bakers.
A welcoming sit-down space,
On the corner where I had stayed.
Adapting a French style, it was so Japanese!
Leaving today, I sincerely bowed at the door.

Kyoto station is modern and enormous
It is fascinating – but so easy to get lost there!
I nearly missed my train, half an hour
Finding number 8277 on a locker.
So easy to mix up the front from the rear of a big station!

I had looked in the guidebook
To find a walk nearby to that ultramodern station.
The Umekoji (Plum Blossom) Park was out of season,
It was the 1001 statues of the Kannon Goddesses of Mercy
Which excited and had my attention.

I had to walk through the busy streets of the centre.
But mobile map apps are annoying
So pretty quickly I had veered in a parallel direction.
Urban art offered a walkway for reflexology,
Paving stones with multiple stimulating textures!

But back to Buddhism and the Sanjusangendo Temple.
I followed a young couple; he is pushing the pram.
We crossed the Kamo river, they turned right.
I carried on, walked up a steep hill,
Turning back to pick up some oranges.

I had noticed the shop, thought
Hmmm, oranges.
So glad I went back!
Inside the shop, it was dark with goods
Mostly on the floor ... some tables.

And there was the old lady, came from the corner
Looked at me and my oranges
And just gave me the most joyous good morning
Ohayōgozaimasu!
You've got to hear it spoken in Japanese to know what I mean!

I had picked them up in a cling film pack.
She just reached and took the oranges from my hand,
Said you don't need this plastic,
Removed them from the packaging, saying
Just have them in your bag!
All done with a flourish, she waved me from her shop
Arigatōgozaimashita … both happy and thanking each other!

I breezed up that hill, thinking,
I must go back and take a picture,
Those meanings so beautifully given.
Turning round I walked the few steps.
I smiled and smiled, repeating *Ohayōgozaimasu!*

About an hour later I headed back for my train.
My head in a spin of 1001 gilt and cypress wood statues.
"Oh My God" … I had gasped in spontaneous awe
As turning a corner in the temple's main hall.
My eyes met the magnificence of the Bodhisattvas,
The Buddha's golden Goddesses of Compassion.

SEIKOKUJI

2022-11-06

I had two nights and one full day in the Seikokuji Buddhist temple. I arrived in the late afternoon after a slow train journey from Kyoto ... the wonders of Kyoto left behind.

I had to change trains – the second train was an enjoyable tourist train – and I was met at a small train station called Yamato Kamiichi on the Kintetsu line. It was a gentle journey, calming me down and preparing me for the arrival at the temple.

The temple monk had arranged for a driver to meet me at Yamato Kamiichi. The station area was very quiet, so creating more calmness as I waited for the car to arrive.

This calmness grew and grew as each moment in Seikokuji passed. When I left, I would say I had become close to a state of serenity – of being calm, peaceful, and untroubled.

The car journey was 35 minutes, so I had the time to look at where I was – on small roads in a Japanese countryside. The driver dropped me off in a small car park by quite a wide river, with high hills covered in forest rising on either side. I stood in the car park and looked around, wondering where to go to find the temple.

I then heard the sound of someone calling out from a distance. I looked up and saw the monk standing up on the hillside on the other side of the road. He shouted to me to come that way ... his voice and manner were friendly.

I walked to where the small temple sat on its own, some 80 steep steps up from the road. The monk showed me where I was staying – in a small, two-storey, modern guesthouse next to the temple.

He showed me my two breakfasts – two bananas and two yoghurts! This was the only food provided – but I had brought some of my own as the temple information had said that there were no meals provided and that there wasn't a nearby shop.

I only saw this monk once more, at the morning prayer. I saw no one else in the temple. It was a place for withdrawing, for quiet and for reflection. And this is what I did.

That evening I did some yoga, having slightly injured my back hurriedly lifting the backpack in Kyoto station earlier that day. It helped.

In the morning, I went into the temple and sat there as the monk went through the chanted prayers. He handed me a small drum with a stick to keep the rhythm as he chanted.

After morning prayer, I went back to my very beautiful, traditional Japanese room. I then left to walk for the rest of the day, with a map showing the paths to two nearby shrines.

The poem begins by describing the encounter with the deer in the forest – one deer screeching to warn the others that I was there. This encounter was at the end of the day, when I had already experienced the meditative calmness of the morning prayer in the temple and the walk along the bank of the river – walking from the temple to a first shrine and then walking back through the forest to a second shrine – where I came across the deer.

The point of view in this poem is of a guest, not of a tourist.
I was a guest not only of the monk and of the temple.
I was also a guest of the beauty of the temple's Japanese aesthetic.

I was a guest of the natural beauty of Japan that I experienced that day – its landscape of a flowing river, its mountains, and its forests.

I was a guest of the river's green pools of water which welcomed me as I sat with my Japanese teaching book, looking down and sitting next to a shrine.

I was a guest of the deer.

I was a guest of the sacred stones that sat by the path in the forest as I walked up to the second shrine.

I was a guest of every sound, smell, sight, and sensation that I experienced that day in Seikokuji.

I wrote my name and address in the book at the shrine, leaving my thanks and my respect as a guest.

Seikokuji is the Temple in Yoshino near Nara where I stayed in its guest house.
Sika is the Japanese deer.
Igirisu is England/UK in Japanese.

Seikokuji

The screech, hurtling out its urgency,
Said look up! It was the sound of a *sika*
Two to three hundred yards away.
Its group, with their brown near black skin
And white flashing rear, scattering
As my scent reached their noses
In a Japanese forest by Seikokuji.

The forest itself sacred, with a path
Only begun at the Temple
And ending at the Shrine.
A 20-minute walk through the skywards pines
To give access to those followers,
Over many hundreds of years
Whom this place had chosen
With its stones carved in greeting
When acknowledging the divine.

I had stayed a night
As a guest in the Temple.
Its Airbnb serving both of us well.
A cloth banner of swimming koi
Hung from the ceiling to the floor.
A tree, from the forest I assumed,
Tactile and decoratively carved
Split the alcove in two.

I had changed into guest green pyjamas,
Beautifully laundered and pressed.
My rucksack having slightly injured my back,
I wore them and did yoga,
Stretched to an iPad recording
From Saleena, my teacher in India!

The information in my room had offered
An invitation to morning prayer.
I sat and shared the thanksgiving,
Beat a drum with a padded stick,
Acknowledged my place
In the manner of the Buddhist sect of Jodo-syu.

I rested, simply walked in the morning
Alongside a shallow, swift flowing river.
The beauty of these surroundings
Reaching to a still warm November sun.
My Japanese language book in my hand
I sat above a pool of green water,
Nature in harmony, having written my legal name
In the blessings book at another shrine
Paul Charlton from Felixstowe, *Igirisu*.

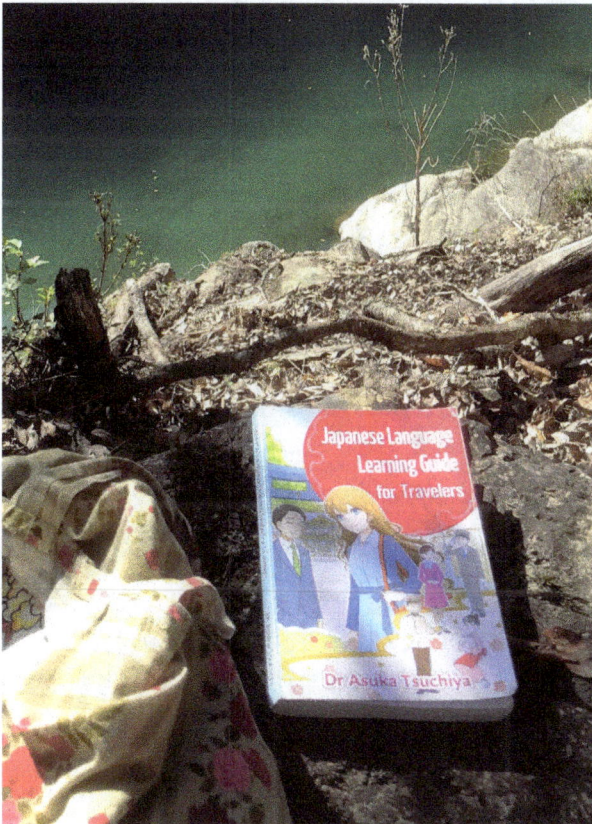

清谷寺

2022年11月6日

　私は清谷寺に2泊して、丸1日をそこで過ごしました。京都から鈍行で、午後遅くに到着……京都の魅力を後にして。

　電車を乗り換えましたが、2番目の電車は楽しい観光電車で、近鉄の大和上市という小さな駅に到着しました。穏やかな旅で、私の気持ちが落ち着き、寺を訪れる準備が整いました。

　僧侶が、大和上市駅まで迎えを寄こしてくれました。駅の辺りはとても静かで、車を待つ間にさらに落ち着いた気持ちになりました。

　清谷寺に滞在している間に、心はますます穏やかになりました。去る時には、とても静穏な境地でした。落ち着き、平和で、心安らかに。

　寺までは車で35分だったので、日本の田舎道の周りを眺める時間がたっぷりありました。運転手が私を下ろした駐車場は、かなり幅の広い川の近くで、両側は木の生い茂る高い丘に囲まれていました。駐車場から周囲を見回しながら、寺はどこだろうと思っていました。

　その時、遠くから誰かが呼ぶ声が聞こえました。見上げると、道の反対側の丘の斜面に僧侶が立っていました。そして私に、こっちに来いと叫んでいました。その声や仕草はとても親近感がありました。

　道から急な階段を80段ほど上ると、小さな寺がポツンと建っていました。僧侶が私の宿泊場所に案内してくれましたが、それは寺の隣にある、小さな2階建てのモダンな宿でした。

　私の2日分の朝食は、2本のバナナとヨーグルト2つ！　これが提供される食物のすべてです。でも寺から、食事は出さないし、近くに店もないと聞いていたので、自分で少し持参していました。

　その後、僧侶に会ったのはたった1度、朝の祈祷の時だけでした。他には誰も見かけませんでした。そこは世間から離れて、静かに内省する場所なのです。私もその通りにしました。

　夕方には、少しヨガをしました。京都駅で急いで荷物を持ち上げた時、少し背

中を痛めたからです。これで楽になりました。

翌朝、私は寺に行って、僧侶が経をあげている間、そこに座っていました。僧侶に小さな太鼓とバチを渡されて、経を唱えている間、リズムを取るようにと言われました。

朝の祈祷の後、私は自分の美しい和室に戻りました。その後、近くの2つの神社への道を記した地図を持って、散歩に出かけました。

この詩は、森での鹿との出会いから始まります。1頭が甲高い声で、私がいることを仲間に警告します。これはその日の最後の出来事で、すでに寺での祈祷で瞑想のような平穏を得て、川辺を散歩した後でした。寺から1つ目の神社まで歩き、それから森を抜けて戻り2つ目の神社に行ったところで、鹿と出会ったのです。

この詩は、観光客ではなく、客人の視点から書いています。

僧侶と寺の客人であるだけではありません。

私は寺の日本美を享受する客人。

また、流れる川や山、森など、その日に堪能した日本の自然の美しさに囲まれた客人でした。

川の緑色の水辺に客人として迎えられ、日本語の教科書を手に、神社の傍に座っていました。

そして鹿にとっての客人。

2つ目の神社に行く途中の森の小道に置かれた神聖な石を訪れた客人でした。

その日、清谷寺で体験したすべての音、香り、見たもの、感じたこと、すべての客人でした

神社で名前と住所を記帳し、客人としての感謝と敬意を示しました。

清谷寺は奈良の近く、吉野にある寺で、私はその宿坊に泊まりました。

清谷寺

甲高い声で緊急事態を知らせる
見ろ！ それは鹿の声
数百メートル先
黒に近い茶色の皮をした群れ
白く光る尻が、パッと散っていく
鼻が私の匂いを察したのか
清谷寺周囲の日本の森

神聖なる森への小道は
寺から始まり
神社で終わる
空にそびえる松林を抜け20分
信者たちの通り道
何百年もの間
この場に選ばれし人々
迎える言葉を石に彫り
聖なるものに出会う

寺の客として
一晩を過ごした
Airbnbでよかった
泳ぐ鯉のぼりが
天井から床まで下がっている
森のものらしき木が
立体的に飾り彫りされ
床の間を2つに仕切る

客用の緑のパジャマに着替える
清潔に洗濯しアイロンがけされている
ラックサックで背中を少し痛めたので
パジャマを着てヨガをする
iPadの録画に合わせてストレッチ
先生のセレーナはインドにいる！

宿の案内によると
朝の祈祷に参加できる
座って感謝を捧げ
布で巻いた棒で太鼓を叩く
この場にふさわしく
浄土宗のしきたりで

私は休み、朝になると散歩をし
流れが速く浅い川に沿って歩く
周りの美しさ
まだ暖かい11月の日差しに手をかざす
日本語の教科書を手に
緑の水溜まりの傍に座る
自然に調和して、自分の名前を書いた
別の神社の芳名帳に
ポール・チャールトン　イギリス、フィーリックストウ 在住

MARINE LINE MISHAP

2022-11-07

This poem pleases me because it praises life in its smallest of details. A ten-second encounter on a train is all it was. But it filled my imagination with joy.

I was part of an accident – a woman falling in my train carriage – and I caught her.

I was travelling from Seikokuji temple to Naoshima, 'the art island'. Two trains to Kyoto; a shinkansen via Osaka to Okayama; a Marine Line train to Takamatsu; and a ferry to Miyanoura on Naoshima.

Travelling on the Marine Line was itself, an accident. I did not know this was a tourist train travelling over a long bridge from the mainland to an island. This bridge gives a wonderful view – but I did not really see it! This was because I was sitting on the lower part of the train which meant the side of the bridge blocked the view.

Three woman my own age had been talking very happily with each other on the Marine Line train journey. Their talking pleased me – it allowed me to listen to the sounds of the Japanese language – not just the phonetics, but the emphasis, the fun, and the communication between them!

However, as the train came into Miyanoura, one of the women stood up from her seat to step down into the train corridor. There was quite a deep step down, so you needed to be careful! I was stepping down in front of her at the same time. The woman then lost her balance and fell into my arms.

She regained her balance immediately and said thank you a number of times. She then carried on leaving the train with her friends.

From Miyanoura Port, I walked across to the other side of the island to my accommodation. The evening light was fading as I walked. But I was still able to walk past and see and experience the beautiful modern art architecture of the Naoshima Elementary School – a modern art designed school!

Later in the evening, I went for a walk by the sea. It was already night and dark with a beautiful moonlit sky – the moon's light shining down and across the sea towards me.

I felt the night scene continuing to connect me to this woman. I wanted to capture this feeling of connection in a poem. The encounter had been of a joyful innocence. The happiness of the three women and the accidental presence of a stranger physically meeting one of them in an embrace.

So much more could have followed from this accident – in another time and in different circumstances. A conversation could have followed which could have changed both our lives – a different path travelled upon forever. Because of a simple encounter.

The poem was written as an expression of a contented connection – written for her, for the sea, and for the moon as a thank you.

Marine Line Mishap

The most exciting thing that happened today
Was when a woman fell into my arms on a train.

I feel as if I should say those lines twice, but then,
I'm travelling at seventy, long past my twenties.

I must have known it was about to happen
As I took this picture of the two storied carriage!

The Marine Line ticket had said CAR 1 SEAT 13-A,
CAR 1 was special, and we were downstairs.

We were travelling Okayama to Takamatsu,
I was catching the ferry to Naoshima Island.

The event itself, was a simple mishap
She fell into the passage as we stood to get off.

It was a full-on loss of balance
My arms reached out and I caught her.

It wasn't a light touch to her shoulders to steady her
It was without doubt – a full on embrace.

She was pleased, not embarrassed,
Just happy I was there, two arms at the ready.

She rapidly repeated, sumi masen, and was on her way.
There were two other friends.

Three older women out for the day
They had no baggage, just laughter and each other.

That evening, I walked along the water's edge
The smell of the sea, the waves gently landing.

The moon, full in the sky, my distant companion.
I thought of her. Wherever she was, we had connected.

I

NAOSHIMA

2022-11-08

This poem describes a whole day and evening on the island of Naoshima. Naoshima is a small island made famous because of its modern art museums, modern art buildings, and public modern art installations.

This was a memorable day for many reasons. I spent the day alone, so was able to absorb the impact of the art slowly and fully. I walked, discovering more of Japan as a place and as a culture – the small shrine at the side of the road, the small and beautifully maintained public garden with a pond, the extraordinary wooden houses with the internal gardens, and the astonishing flower arrangements just at a front door!

But! Naoshima is a modern construction, with modern attitudes and modern visitors. It unsettled me. This unsettled feeling was because at times I felt I was actually in a European city with its wealth and expensive objects for sale.

This poem therefore expresses this contradiction between the astonishing, traditional Japanese beauty of the flowers in their pot and the astonishing beauty of the Monet painting in the consumerism of a modern museum – the design, as well, by a celebrated Japanese architect.

On the personal level, the day was so clear and warm – with a stunning blue sky and an uninterrupted view of everything. I lay on the grass outside the museum with the Monet painting, looking across the water at the town of Takamatsu … the sea smooth as glass. A group of young people laughed when they saw me on the grass with my hat covering my face in the sun – amused by seeing me lying full out and lazily resting.

In the morning, I left the old guest house to walk around the old part of the small harbour town. I talk about the guest house in the poem. It was not traditional – almost like a hostel with almost no facilities and no food or drink available. The room had one plate and one knife and one spoon etc. It was rather odd – as if the owners had given up after a very long time of caring for guests and wanted to stop.

The guest house though was situated within the old streets – its back gate opened onto the road by the sea and the fishing boats. It was here that I walked along the narrow streets with their old wooden houses and where I heard the two women talking inside one of them – sounding like a mother and daughter – and I wondered what they were talking about!

I saw the astonishing flowerpot with its beautifully made arrangements of flowers and plants – outrageous to just be sitting in the doorway of someone's ordinary house!

And so too I saw and stood and looked with amazement at the exquisite internal gardens and courtyards of these houses – Japanese at its most essential, I felt.

I walked from these houses to the small museum honouring Tadao Ando, the architect of the modern art museum I would visit later that day. From there I found the eccentric cafe, Konichiwa, and had a coffee and chocolate cake.

Rested, I walked to the Chichu Art Museum. I was utterly unprepared for the painting by Monet. It is enormous! It is like looking at a film in a cinema … it was the only painting in the room. The room is cleverly designed to allow the painting to open up as you walk through the entrance and to land in front of it, entranced and awed by its magnificence!

The other artists I talk about in the poem as well – so modern and provocative of my senses!

The combination of art, the wooden houses and their gardens and flowers with the very rare red moon and the red pomegranate on its tree approached the miraculous!

Red Moon, Monet, and a Red Pomegranate Tree

Part One

I'm more than a bit bewildered by today.
It's been contrasts and contradictions,
Monet! Lilies In a Pond!

Utterly overwhelmed by the setting of his painting
A museum underground, a concrete exhibition room.
A V-shaped entrance captures his painting at its point
You are stunned and you stand there
And see a wall full-length of Monet's intent
One of five especially chosen for this setting.

An indisputable temple to modern art,
Chichu Art Museum, Naoshima Island,
Tadao Ando, the mighty architect.

Two more names, only familiar today,
James Turrell and Walter De Maria
Exhibit with Monet as a trio.
No clutter, just those three.

My friend David Anstey stood a whole morning
Just gazing at one painting in Amsterdam.
He said he couldn't bear to move to look at another
He was looking at a Monet.

My bewilderment in part lies in what he said
I need days to recover and understand what I just saw.

Walter De Maria

In his space,
An amphitheatre,
He placed a 2.2 metre diameter sphere.
Set onto the walls
Were 27 wooden sculptures
Covered with gold leaves.
Above, a window to the sky.

Mesmerised.

James Turrell

His three works present light
As art.
Barely able to see
A guide leads through a haze
Up steps,
An atrium, pale blue.

Made sense less.

Fortunately, I was walking
So could retrace my steps back
Past the museum garden – designed in the style of Monet.
So bewilderingly contradictory,
So European.

This is Naoshima.

Part Two

I had got up fairly early, completing yesterday's poem.
A personal encounter, unlike today.
The guest house is called Oomiyake,
The main part 400 years old.
The Miyake family, the 'Oo' an honorific
Meaning grand or great.

It sits in a street of other old wooden houses
I walked and looked and listened to their stories.
Inside one of their doorways
Was an exquisite Japanese garden
Green moss, shapely shining green trees,
Cut stones for paving, and a standing stone hare.
A Buddhist icon, or just modern flair!

Inside, I could hear a conversation,
Two women, one older and the other younger.
Not understanding creates a subjective silence,
My imagination intuiting that much more.

As I wandered along, the flowerpot
Stood there, outrageous.
There has to be another word than beautiful.
Was that hours or moments to make?
I have no idea.
How dare it just be there
Be just at someone's door.

Shortly after the pot,
I visited the Tadao Ando personal museum,
The afternoon's modern art was later.
It was a good time for coffee,
I had seen a café earlier, not yet open,
Café Konichiwa.
It gave me my first postcard,
As well as coffee, and a sugar bowl
Sitting in a crocheted case ...

An hour later, I was rested and left.
That is how I happened
To notice the red pomegranate
Clustered with others on a tree
Looking as if it was there forever and eternity.

The proof of that
Was the red moon in the sky
As I walked out in the evening.
A rare celestial event not seen in 442 years.
When a total lunar eclipse
Hides Uranus from view
And the planet is eclipsed by the moon.

This is Naoshima.

NAOSHIMA TWO

2022-11-10

A Huge Cat!

I wrote this poem on the train on the way from Naoshima to Hiroshima.

It was a reflection on the previous day – a second full day looking at modern art in a different but equally provocative museum. By provocative I mean a museum where the art forces itself upon you and informs your understanding of everything.

As I said about the poem the day before, Naoshima confused me. It makes you stand both in the East and in the West.

Of course, I am deeply thankful that I went there as the art I describe in the poem truly moved me in a way I had not experienced for many decades.

I sailed on a small boat from the island to a different port than the one I had arrived from. This port was Uno. Walking from the boat to Uno station, you walk by a wide-open park. In the centre of this modern park made of concrete and grass is a very large, modern but almost classical sculpture, made with 2.7 x 2 x 2 meters of Chinese granite.

I walked across to the sculpture and looked at it closely. It is a representation of a woman with intertwining limbs in an open pose – the sculptor Dhruva Mistry, a celebrated Indian artist – the sculpture titled "The Goddess of Love".

The sculpture was commissioned as part of the intention to create a modern art landscape approaching Naoshima – to prepare the visitor for the island itself.

The experience of this sculpture came with me onto the train and led the poem. Before that was the sense of relief as I got on the boat to leave the island – needing to be back in the East – in Japan.

As I have said however – I was grateful to the island and its momentous art. I did eat beautiful food – a sashimi main meal – in a small restaurant with one person only working. He was the cook and the waiter. I sat on the floor for the first time. I slowly drank a small flask of sake after the meal – content.

The poem's artworks are:

- *Pacific* by Yukinori Yanagi
- *Three Chattering Men* by Jonathan Borofsky
- *The Bloodline* by Zhang Xiaogang
- *Three Squares Vertical Diagonal* by George Rickey
- *Cat* by Niki de Saint Phalle

A Huge Cat!

A sense of relief to leave Naoshima.
In spite of the settings and the Monet,
An uncomfortable sense of service
Leant more to the corporate,
Than the Yamaguchi sake
Drank with last night's local sashimi,
When, for the first time, I sat on a mat
And ate comfortably on the floor.

I'm on a boat, it's eight in the morning
And I'm on my way to Hiroshima.

So, to go back on myself, and contradict,
I really adored yesterday's artwork.
Unlike the grandeur of the day before,
This Benesse House Museum was full of doom!
A wall full of neatly positioned national flags
Each one scarred and broken through
By the action of unrelenting ants.

Standing opposite three mechanical human figures.
Metallic – programmed with sounds sending you crazy.
They were chilling, those "Chattering Figures".

And a Bloodline painting by a Chinese genius,
A man and a woman, she at home, he a party functionary,
Their younger selves positioned alongside,
Bloodline replicas, identities of a Cultural Revolution.

And outside on a grassy knoll,
Three moving, amusing metal plates
Invited the gaze to the unbroken blue landscape
Of a summer in November's sea and its sun.

I laid on that knoll and rested flat on my back,
Some women passing by were caught by surprise
Breaking into laughter
My Swiss cap at an angle over my eyes.

And of course, there was the cat.
A ridiculous giant, no apologies for public art.
But you had to look at it, not think too much,
Just love it.

In the same vein, I loved the municipal humour.
A sign, fixed to a rail at steps down to the sand,
Offered its message adorned by a graphic design
Within a border of five-petalled flowers,
Perhaps that pink yaeda we met in Nagoya.
Above the clouds at the top of the notice
Was a flying pink tin can!
The words on this notice an environmentalist's dream:
"Everyone's town can stay beautiful
When neither left nor right hand
Throws away our trash".

I'm now on a train from Uno to Okayama
Local and yellow with 14 stops to go.
Outside the station the area was open and flat.
Attracting your look was a statue stood alone,
A figure of a woman, made of Chinese granite.
She drew me across as she was powerful.
Intertwined limbs and expression exposed
"The Goddess of Love", the sculptor Dhruva Mistry.

HIROSHIMA

The Dome
2022-11-10

My intention in coming to Hiroshima was to apologise for my shared action in the use of the atomic bomb in 1945. Using the atomic bomb at Hiroshima is, and always will be, a shared action of every human being. Our capacity as humans caused this to happen.

It is equally an obligation to apologise at the Auschwitz extermination camp as it is to apologise at Hiroshima.

I arrived in Hiroshima in the afternoon of 10th November. My plan was to stay for two nights. In my mind had been the thought that if I stayed the two nights only then I would avoid the act of spectating, as if in an art museum.

I would witness the site of this shameful event, apologise, and leave.

I left my backpack at the train station, leaving by a large underground space of modern marble and peace dove ceramic tiles. I walked a little to locate myself at rest, no longer travelling. On the corner of a small public space was a baker shop, where I enjoyed the ambience and bought something to eat. I sat by the space for a while before walking back to the station to find a bus to the Peace Memorial Park.

But it wasn't a bus I found, it was a tram – a modern tram, not like the one I caught back. I enjoyed sitting on this tram with its large views of the street and the opportunity to look at the people sitting and standing inside.

So, I was calm when the tram arrived at the stop for the Peace Memorial Park. It was late afternoon, and it was sunny and pleasant. I stepped off the tram and walked a few steps before going onto the pavement with other passengers moving to the park. I wasn't looking about in any real sense as to where I was going.

It was on the wide pavement, before I noticed the park, that I was approached by the woman with her leaflets and words saying, 'Buddha is the one'. I welcomed her words and bowed, then moved away, looking up as I did. And it was then that I realised I was almost already in the park.

And in the moment as I looked up, I saw the Dome. It was very near, in full sight. I was shocked – unprepared – and I immediately began to cry at the meaning of what was before my eyes. This was The Hiroshima Peace Memorial, also known as the Genbaku Dome, made up of the structure of the only building left standing near the place where the first atomic bomb exploded on August 6, 1945.

I moved to the side, where there was a very low wall with a hedge running beside it – the edge of the park by the pavement. I sat on the wall and began to recover. As I did, the sun's orb appeared within the foliage of the tree, casting the dome in an extraordinary light. It made me think immediately of the light from the atomic blast and the tens of thousands of instantaneous deaths that it precipitated.

The appearance of the children then created this most perfect balance of past, present, and future as I sat.

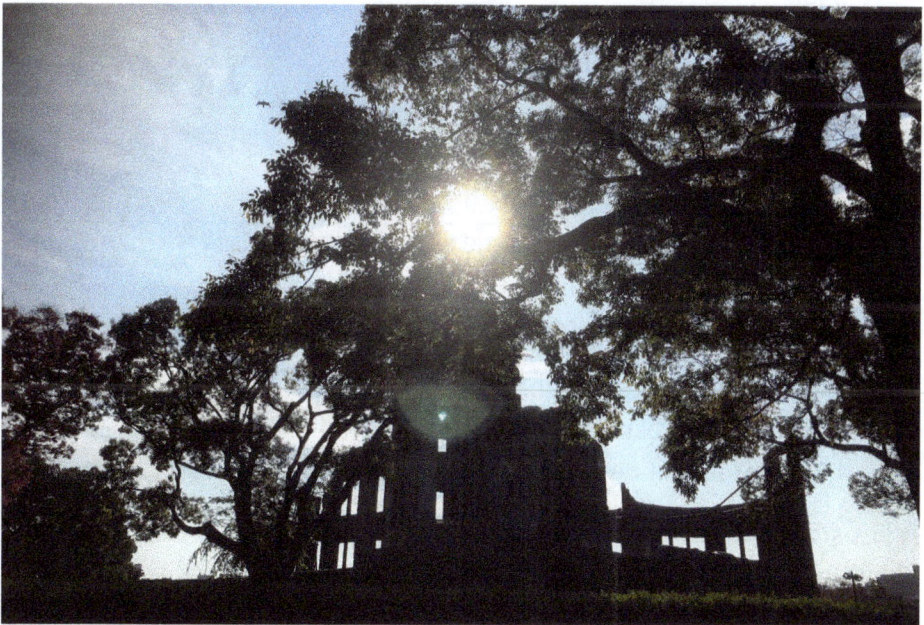

Hiroshima One

The Dome

How is it possible not to cry?

I wasn't prepared.

I came over a crossing from an electric tram.
Three women were in front of me, one of whom
Had a neat phone bag round her shoulder
Which I was admiring.

On the pavement, a step toward the park,
A smiling woman with a broad brimmed hat
Stepped in front of me and handed me a paper.
'Buddha,' she said.
She was proselytising.

She translated by speaking into her app …
'Buddha is the one.'

A second step and before I could look up,
The dome instead was looking down on me.
It was like a shock wave to my system,
I burst into tears.

Nothing can prepare for the significance of the dome.
Earlier, I had walked across the Enko-bashi bridge
Its structure left standing after the blast,
It had carried the survivors from one side to the other.
The catastrophic sense of those feet on the ground
Had first brought the tear I could no longer hold back.

A group of black uniformed schoolgirls
Gathered around a freshwater tap,
The trip to this park a necessary part of their growing up.

A low stone wall offers me a seat.
I leant back against the hedge
Grateful for the chance for my body to safely sit.

Still shaking, I glanced up again.
The afternoon sun was lowering in the sky
Its orb striking light through every window of the ruin.
It's too obvious, but is that the last so many felt
As an A-bomb's arc exploded over Hiroshima
On August 6, 1945.
One light, one cloud, a rush of heat,
A rumbling heard many miles away.
Up to 80,000 dead as a result.

Then gorgeously,

Five mothers and about the same number of young children,
(there were seven, and one of the women was pregnant)
Were standing in front of me.
The little ones had found perhaps a squirrel
And were running along the wall,
Excitedly jumping up and jumping down
To get around me!
Hai, future generations have come
And we are all an amazing part of continuing our stories.

Today in the park, is to come and bow our heads
And for us all to ask for forgiveness for yesterday.

広島

ドーム
2022年11月10日

　広島を訪れたのは、1945年に原爆を投下した行為を、我がこととして謝罪するためです。広島への原爆投下は、いつまでも、人類すべての責任です。人間の能力が引き起こしたことなのです。

　アウシュビッツ強制収容所のことを謝罪するのと同じように、広島にも謝らなくてはなりません。

　広島に到着したのは11月10日の午後でした。2泊の予定でした。2泊だけなら、美術館のように鑑賞するような愚行を避けられると思ったのです。

　恥ずべき出来事のあった場所を目撃し、謝罪したら、立ち去ろうと。

　駅に荷物を預け、通り抜けた広い地下の空間は、現代的な大理石と平和の鳩のタイル張りでした。少し歩いたら、旅の疲れを休めることにしました。小さな公共スペースの角にパン屋があったので、少しのんびりして食べ物を買いました。しばらく座った後、駅の方に歩いて戻り、平和記念公園行きのバスを探しました。

　でも見つけたのはバスではなく、路面電車でした。往路は現代的な路面電車で、復路とは違いました。私は座席に座って、大きな窓からの通りの眺めや、車内の乗客を見る機会に恵まれました。

　だから路面電車が平和記念公園に到着した時、私はとても心が落ち着いていました。晴れていて気持ちが良い午後でした。路面電車を降りて数歩で歩道に出て、他の乗客と共に、平和記念公園に向かいました。どこに向かうのか、見回すこともありませんでした。

　その歩道は広く、公園だとわからぬうちに、チラシを持った女性が私に近づいてきて、「即心是仏」と言いました。私はその言葉を受け止め、お辞儀をして、通り過ぎ、目をあげました。その時、もう公園だと気づいたのです。

　目を上げた瞬間に、ドームがありました。とても近く、全貌が見えました。それがショックでした。予期していなかったのです。そして目の前にあるものの意味を悟ると、すぐ涙が出てきました。これが広島平和記念碑、またの名は原爆ドーム。1945年8月6日に初めて原爆が投下された爆心地の近くで、唯一残った建

物の骨組みなのです。

　歩道の脇に寄ると、低い壁に沿って生垣がありました。歩道は、公園の境にあったのです。私はその低い壁に座って、落ち着きを取り戻しました。その時、太陽が木々の茂みから現れ、類稀なる光をドームに落としました。それは、一瞬にして何万人もの命を奪った原爆の光線を思わせました。

　座っている私の目の前に、子供たちが現れ、過去と現在と未来のバランスを見事に示す光景が広がりました。

広島　1

ドーム

泣かずにいられるだろうか？

心の準備ができていなかった

路面電車を降り、横断歩道を渡ると
前にいた3人の女性の1人が
携帯電話を肩から下げている
そのバッグに目を奪われていた

公園に向かう歩道で
つばの広い帽子をかぶった笑顔の女性が
私の前に立ち止まり、紙を手渡しながら
「仏様」と言う
布教をしているのだ

彼女が翻訳アプリに話しかける
「即心是仏」

2歩進み、私が目を上げる前に
ドームが見下ろしていた
衝撃の波が体を襲い
涙が溢れた

このドームの重さを受けとめられない
ここに来る前に、猿猴橋を渡った
爆風にも耐え残った橋

生き残った人々を対岸に渡した橋
その時の惨状を思うと
涙をこらえられなかった

黒い制服の女子学生たちが
水飲み場の近くに集まっている
この公園への修学旅行は、大人になるのに必要な過程

私は低い石垣に座らせてもらう
生垣にもたれて
体を委ねられることに感謝
まだ震えながら、再び目を上げる
午後の陽の光は低くなってゆく
その日差しが、廃墟のあらゆる窓を照らす
言うまでもなく、あの最後の光を思う
広島に原爆が投下された
1945年8月6日
ひとつの光、ひとつの雲、押し寄せる熱波
何キロも先で聞こえた爆音
8万人が命を落とした

だがまばゆいことに

5人の母親が小さな子供たちを連れて
（子供は7人、女性の1人は身重）
私の前に立っている
子供たちは、リスを見つけたのか
壁に沿って走っている
興奮してぴょんぴょん跳ね
私に近づいてくる！
はい、未来の世代到来
誰もが大事な役割を担い、物語は続く

今日は公園に頭を下げに来た
昨日を許してもらうために

HIROSHIMA TWO

A Couple on a Tram
2022-11-10

I left the Peace Memorial Park at 3.30pm – unable to move forward into the park from my seat on the wall where the dome had pressed, and the children had played. The effect of the sorrow I had felt had overwhelmed and there was no room in my head for new images and thoughts.

I waited at the same tram stop as I had descended – if in the other direction – to get back to the train station where my bag was in its locker. The tram this time was an old green and cream coloured one, number 1901, built in 1957 in Kyoto before arriving in Hiroshima in 1978. I was immediately reconnected with another time, not modern and closer to my state of mind as I sat down on a bench running along the centre side of the tram.

The same bench was opposite me and sitting on that was a couple in their late twenties. She was asleep, fallen into him with unconditioned trust. He was tired too but sat up, awake and aware of her. They stood out, like a living artwork which imposes itself upon you and demands that you take notice.

I projected my own reflected and sombre mood upon them, wondering what their circumstances were – where they were coming from and going to. They were dressed as if their journey or their work had been hard. But overwhelmingly, their combined posture expressed a love for each other which was clear and powerful, and which made me wish them well. It was a further affirmation, after witnessing the children play, of how we should be, as comforting one another and not harming each other.

A Couple on a Tram

She was sleeping,
Her hand lying lightly in the palm of his.
Her body rested against his completely
Her chest moved in and out deeply,
Unusually so for a short nap on a tram.
Seeming runaways with just each other,
There wasn't a molecule of air between them.
Though tired too, he kept awake
Aware of the need as to when to get off.

She was wearing a thin coat
On her feet, light slipper shoes.
If she were older, I would have said she was ill.
But no, she was strong, merely exhausted,
Hard work they shared, or just the journey they were making,
He was poorly dressed too.
By that I mean their clothes were meagre,
Perhaps from a market stall and well worn.
They were out of place,
His eyes didn't challenge but he noticed me looking.

They presented the most deeply felt love.
He, feather light, moved his left hand on hers
Indicating they were nearing a stop
Requesting that she should waken.
She didn't really respond, remained deeply breathing
He didn't persist, he knew her rest was needed.

They were young, less than thirty,
Whatever it was that caused their isolation
It would have been hard it seemed to me.
As it wasn't just fatigue, it was ageing
That wore into their appearance.
His eyes not searching beyond themselves
Her feet turned to his, folds around her ankles.

They were proud, in spite of which
I wanted to lean over and offer them money.
I did the maths in my head
Multiplying 1000 yen into sterling
And thought 40 million.
I even imagined an envelope handed over.
Saying this is for you, please take it.

He more pressingly asked her to come awake
Used his voice now, gentle, never losing any
Of their whole-body contact.
She rose with him from the seat they were on
A long bench for half a dozen, directly opposite.
Still not alert, her hand, once stood up, kept to his,
The tram swayed and momentarily they were separated.
They closed the gap, she moved back into him
Their fingers didn't intertwine, her palm
Laid across the back of his, as they leant in together.

They disappeared from the tram
I didn't really see them onto the pavement
I was desperate to wish them well.
Their stop, one before the terminus at Hiroshima station,
Even that I thought unusual.

広島　2

路面電車のふたり
2022年11月10日

　平和記念公園を出たのは3時半でした。ドームの近く、子供たちが遊んでいたところで、石垣に座ったまま、先に進むことができなかったのです。あまりに圧倒的な悲しみで、それ以上は何も見たり考えたりする余裕がありませんでした。

　私は先ほど降車した路面電車の停留所で、別方向の電車を待ちました。駅のロッカーに残したバッグを取りに戻るためです。今度乗るのは、緑とクリーム色で、1957年に京都で製造され、1978年に広島にきた旧車両の1901号です。車両の両サイドにある座席につくとすぐに、心が異なる時空へと繋がりました。そこは現代ではなく、もっと私の心情に近い時代でした。

　私の向かい側に座っていたのは、20代後半のカップルでした。女性は眠っていて、男性を無条件に信頼して寄りかかっていました。彼も疲れているようですが、きちんと座り、眠らずに彼女に気を配っています。二人はあたかも生きている芸術作品のように、目を引きました。

私は自分の内省的で重苦しい気持ちを投影し、彼らはどういう状況なのか考えました。どこからきて、どこに行くのだろうと。身なりから、何か大変な旅かきつい仕事の後のように見えました。でも何よりも、寄り添い合う姿に表れるお互いへの愛情が、あまりにも明確で力強いので、幸運を祈らずにいられませんでした。子供たちが遊ぶのを見た後だっただけに、私たちのあるべき姿は、お互いに慰め合うことであって、傷つけあう事ではないのだと、さらに確信したのでした。

路面電車のふたり

彼女は眠っている
その手を、彼の手のひらに軽くのせて
体をすっかり預けて
深い息づかいで胸が上下する
路面電車の短い居眠りなのに
2人だけで逃げてきたのか
お互いの間にわずかな隙間もない
疲れているだろうに、彼は眠らない
いつ降りるか気を配っている

彼女は薄手のコートを着ている
足元は軽いスリッポンの靴
これで若くなければ、病気かと心配なところ
でも違う、彼女は強く、ただ疲れているだけ
一緒にしたきつい仕事のせいか
共に歩んでいる困難な旅のせいか
彼も身なりはよくない
つまり貧相な服装で
市場で買ったのか、着倒したのか
どこか場違いで
私が見ていると気づいても、彼の目に変化はない

ふたりは深い愛情を表している
彼は左手で、羽のように軽く彼女の手に触れて
もうすぐ降車駅だから
起きろとうながす
彼女は応えず、変わらぬ深い息づかい
彼は無理強いしない。休息が必要だから

彼らは若く、30歳にも満たない
孤立した理由は何であれ
辛かったのだろうと思わせる
疲れているだけでなく、その年のとり方
容姿に表れている
彼の目はこれ以上のものを求めない
彼女は足首を組み、足は彼の方を向いている

自尊心はあるだろう
それなのに私は身を乗り出して
お金をあげたくなる
頭で計算する
1000円をポンドで換算し
4千万になる
封筒を渡すことまで考えた
君たちのものだ、受け取ってくれと言いつつ

彼は、起きろと少し強くうながす
今度は声に出し、優しく
体はぴったりつけたまま
彼女は一緒に、座席から立ち上がる
私の向かい側の、長い6人がけの座席
まだぼんやりと、彼女の手は
立ち上がっても彼の手の中
路面電車が揺れて、一瞬離れた
でもすぐ近づき、手は彼の元に戻る
指を絡めることはなく
彼女の手のひらは、彼の手の甲に触れ
もたれあう

やがて2人は電車を後にする
歩道での様子は見なかった
元気でいてほしいと切に願う
終点の広島駅の1駅手前で降車
それさえも何か違うように思えた

HIROSHIMA THREE

IN MEMORIAM Hiroshima Prefectural
First Girls' High School
2022-11-11

This poem doesn't really need an account of how it was written, or how I felt, or what happened on the day, whose point of view, or its connections with other events.

As the first line says, I left the hotel that morning full of apprehension as I anticipated the profound sorrow I was to experience before the day ended. I wrote the poem as the day went from one point of sorrow to the next. The first point reached very quickly after leaving the hotel as I stood before a memorial for the school children of Hiroshima Prefectural First Girls' High School destroyed by the bomb.

The poem's first lines were written as I rested from the weight of the morning's witness. Then finished in the evening as I lay exhausted and ready to leave the following morning – so as to tell this poem's story to as many people as I possibly could, for as many days that I could possibly live.

Gomen nasai is a phrase conveying an apology.
Arigatougozaimasu means thank you.

IN MEMORIAM Hiroshima Prefectural First Girls' High School

I left the hotel this morning full of apprehension.
As I walked down Hiroshima's busy Peace Boulevard
A school and its children the first awful memorial I passed.

I am sat on a bench outside an exhibit space
Inside was the floor of someone's home
Incinerated, melted, a neighbour's account horrifying.

Endless children pass in lines
I admire their fortitude, or is it of their teachers
Who class after class, and year after year
Revisit and explain again their city's sorrowing.

Two workers sweep the leaves towards where I sit
The dust rises up and mixes with my tears.
I stand up to go, *'gomen nasai',* one of them says.
Concerned it was because of their sweeping.

A few steps and a sign in blue is inviting me in.
Hiroshima National Memorial Hall for the Atomic Bomb Victims.
Before I do, I pass the leaf sweeper again
I approach her and bend saying *'gomen nasai,*
Arigatougozaimasu'. It is me who is grateful.
She smiles and bows, brightened by my words.

I'm crying again, this time, so are others.
The Memorial Hall has the name of every single person
Known to have died following the atomic blast.
Its centrepiece, a circular room, shows the bombed Hiroshima.
Every destroyed district mentioned by place name
In a 360-degree pictorial, and a water clock
Showing the time as 8.15, at the centre.

A panel of photographs is in constant motion
They are the pictures and identities of the victims.
Still today you can register, and so it continues.
I spoke with a woman at the Tourist Information Centre.
She said that the name of her great grandmother was inside,
As were five other members of her family.

The Memorial Hall exhibition is called Trembling Gazes.
The account of photographers there at the time,
"Their words born from gazing upon destruction."
We sat and listened to the words of the men themselves,
Some accidental survivors, protected by a wall,
Others as relief workers, one, a day off.
Another, a father whose child went early to school.
He found her on a bridge, trying to make her way back,
Her body brutally damaged. She died, aged 8, a few hours later.
He was asked to take photos of the damaged power lines,
He said this took him to a rooftop and for the next coming years
He took photos of Hiroshima's rebuilding.
The demand of his daughter, he said,
To make this record for us to see
To be reminded that never again
Should humans use this power of destruction.

The Peace Park has a rest area and a café, to recover.
But still, it too doesn't let you escape
As in front of you and your coffee is Akiko's piano.
She was 19 and one kilometre from the hypocentre,
When the atomic bomb was dropped on the city.
She died next day from acute radiation sickness.
Her piano survived, though scarred by glass fragments
Restored 60 years later, to perform peace themed music.

I had remained a long time by the memorial for the children.
This is the story of the 1000 paper cranes carefully folded
By the child believing with all those made
Her wish would come true, and she would live.
At age 12, Sadako Sasako died of leukaemia.

A woman stood alongside turned and spoke.
She said, where was I from, all of this in English.
She was a teacher, there with her class,
One of them, a boy, gave me his workbook.
We spoke a while excitedly,
What more could I have asked for than this conversation?

The children's memorial has a bell
To be pulled and rung for remembering.
So, it was noisy as we talked.
She was very happy to know
I was so long in Japan,
A greeting made more emphatic
At a shared affection for the poems of Kaneko Misuzu.

I said I had earlier written in a poem
Of my admiration for the teachers.
She asked if she could see it, so I read it as it was.
The pain of these records repeated again and again
As a demand to not forget.

I didn't know about the 20,000 Koreans
Who died that day or sometime later.
By the mound of the ashes of Hiroshima's 70,000 citizens,
Whose ashes lie identified and gathered together,
There is a monument with a turtle at the base
And with two dragons astride at the top.
The description given ...
The Korean victims were given no funerals.
And their spirits hovered for years,
Unable to pass onto heaven ...
This monument was erected in the hope
That the souls of our compatriots,
Brought to misery through force,
Will be able to rest in peace.

Thankfully, I had left to the end of the day
The visit to the Peace Memorial Museum.
Personal story upon story, pain upon pain.
It is unbearable when in your heart and in your soul
You too have a parent, a child, a brother, a sister,
A grandfather, a grandmother, a husband, a wife.

Hiroshima Prefectural First Girls' High School,
Collapsed in the blast and burnt completely.
Twenty teachers and two hundred and eighty-one students.
Part of their monument
Is a heart shaped frame for paper cranes.
These ones made by a women's group from Takasaki,
A town northwest of Tokyo.

The school emblem is engraved on the monument.
It is a heart.

広島　3

追憶 広島県立広島第一高等女学校
2022年11月11日

　この詩は、どのように書いたのか、どう感じたのか、その日何があったのか、誰の視点なのか、他の出来事との関わりなど、説明する必要はおそらくないでしょう。

　1行目にあるように、朝ホテルを出た時から、その日が終わるまで深い悲しみを感じることはわかっていました。この詩を書いたのは、ひとつの悲しみから、次の悲しみへと移ったことを書いたものです。まずホテルを出てすぐに、原爆で全壊した広島県立広島第一高等女学校の生徒たちの追憶碑の前に立っていました。

　この詩のはじめの数行は、その朝見たことのあまりの重さに、休憩した時に書きました。詩を書き終えた夕方には疲れ果てて横になり、翌朝に去る支度を終えていました。そして私が生きている限り、できるだけ多くの人々に、この詩の物語を伝えようと思ったのです。

追憶　広島県立広島第一高等女学校

朝ホテルを出た時から、不安が募った
広島の、人通りの多い平和通りを歩いて行くと
最初に通りかかるのは、学校とその生徒たちの恐ろしい追悼碑

展示場の外のベンチに座った
中は誰かの住まいだった
焼け、溶け、近所の人の恐ろしい思い出

数えきれない子供たちの列が通り過ぎる
子供たち、いや教師たちの、不屈の精神に感心する
毎年、次から次へと違う学級と
何度も訪れ、街の悲しみを説明し続ける

私が座っていると、2人の清掃人が落ち葉を掃いた
埃がのぼり、涙に混ざる
私が立ち上がると、1人が「ごめんなさい」と言う
掃除のせいだと心配したのだ

数歩先で、青い看板が私を招いている
国立広島原爆死没者追悼平和祈念館
入る前に、また清掃人たちを通り過ぎる
私は近づいて腰を曲げつつ、「ゴメンナサイ」
「アリガトウゴザイマス」と言う
感謝するのは私だ
彼女は嬉しそうに、微笑みお辞儀をする

私はまた泣いてしまう、今回は他の人も一緒に
祈念館にはひとりひとりの名前が
すべて記録されている
判明している原爆死没者の人たち
中央の円形の追悼空間には、被爆直後の広島の様子
破壊された地域のすべての名前
360度のパノラマ
中央で、水時計が8時15分を示す

写真パネルは常に動いている
続々と現れる犠牲者の写真と名前
今もまだ登録が続いている
観光局の女性と話をした
彼女のひいおばあさんの名前もあるそうだ
他にも5人の親族の名

メモリアルホールの展示の題は「震えるまなざし 」
当時広島にいた撮影者たちが
"惨状を見つめ紡いだ言葉"
座って当事者の言葉を聞いた
ある人は壁によって守られ、奇跡的に生き延びた
救援者たち、休暇中だった人
または、早めに学校に行った子供のお父さん
帰宅しようとしていた娘を、途中の橋で見つけた
無残な姿の娘は、8歳で数時間後に亡くなった
彼は、破損した電線の写真撮影を依頼された
屋根に上がり、その後何年も
広島の復興を撮影し続けた
娘に頼まれたと、彼は言う

この記録を見てもらえるように
こんなことが2度と起きないように
人類がこの破壊力を使わないように

平和公園には休憩所やカフェがあり、気を持ち直すことができる
でも逃れることはできない
コーヒーの向こう側に、明子さんのピアノが見える
街に原爆が落ちた時、彼女は19歳
爆心地から1キロのところにいた
翌日急性放射線症で亡くなった
彼女のピアノは、ガラスの破片で傷つきながらも残った
60年後に修復され、平和をテーマとした音楽が演奏される。

私は長い間、原爆の子の像 の前にいた
丁寧に折られた千羽鶴の物語
鶴を折れば
願いが叶い、生きていけると思った子
佐々木禎子さんは12歳で白血病で亡くなった

そばに立っていた女性が話しかけてきた
どこからきたのか、英語で問われる
彼女は教師で、担任する学級と来ていた
1人の男の子が、私にワークブックをくれた
しばらく興奮して話した
この会話以上のものが望めるだろうか

原爆の子の像には鐘がある
紐を引くと鐘がなり、あの日を思い出す
だから、話している間は音がなり続けた
私が日本に長期旅行中と聞いて
彼女はとても喜んでくれた
さらに盛り上がったのは
ふたりとも金子みすゞの詩を愛していたから

教師たちへの畏敬の念を
以前詩に書いたことがある
それが見たいと言われ、朗読した
何度も繰り返される記憶の痛み
忘れさせないために

私は知らなかった、2万人の韓国人たちが
あの日、そしてその後に、亡くなったことを
広島市民7万人の遺灰が
集められた山の傍に
亀の土台の慰霊碑があり
てっぺんでは2匹の龍が天に昇る
碑文によると
「韓国人の犠牲者は誰からも供養を受けることなく
その魂は永く
さまよい続けていた
この碑が県立されたのは
悲惨を強いられた
同胞の霊を安らげ
原爆の惨事を二度とくりかえないため」

平和祈念館の訪問が
その日の最後の予定だったのは幸いだ
次々に人々の物語、痛みが続き
私の心と魂が耐えられない
誰しも、両親や子供、兄弟や姉妹
祖父母、夫、妻がある

広島県立広島第一高等女学校は
爆風で崩壊し全焼した
20人の教師と281名の生徒たち
慰霊碑の一部は
ハート型の額に入った折り鶴
東京から北西に位置する高崎という街の
女性たちが作成したものだという

追憶の碑に刻まれている学校の紋章は
ハート型だ

ENJOYING YAMAGUCHI

2022-11-12

I hadn't intended to visit Yamaguchi – some 100 km to the south of Hiroshima. It was where I was catching a bus to cross over the central Japan mountain range – so it was to have been a walk out of the train station and a wait in a bus station. I had planned to catch a local bus from Yamaguchi to Hagi on the coast of the Sea of Japan. The local bus was so I could take my time to look out of the slow-moving bus as it travelled across the mountain range and through its villages.

What happened instead, was a mix up of train stations resulting in a wonderful day wandering around Yamaguchi's covered shopping arcade – a *shōtengai*.

I was to find two more of these Japanese arcades called *shōtengai*, one in Hagi and the other in Himeji. These traditional shopping arcades are fascinating, each with their own unique specialties, atmosphere, and character. I spent a few beautiful hours awed and entertained by the stretching glass roofs, old shops, and people in the Yamaguchi *shōtengai*.

I begin this poem praising the good fortune that had been with me every day in Japan. Good fortune which was far more valuable than the money I had saved and borrowed from the bank to get me here!

At Hiroshima's station, I succeeded in buying the shinkansen train seat reservation to Yamaguchi, speaking a little of the very little Japanese I was more confident in using. Then and later at Shin Yamaguchi train station, I encountered the unconditioned generosity from the beautiful people who helped me find my way to Hagi!

Enjoying Yamaguchi

I had no hesitation in taking all the money I could
From the banks before I left!
But the good fortune that has been with me
Every day since I came to Japan
Has surpassed by far the exchange rate of my yen.

Take today, or *'kyo'* in Japanese!
Yes, I said *'kyo'* at the ticket office for the train
Japan Rail's magic 28-day JR Pass in my hand.
Before I knew it, I was on the 10:35 Shinkansen
To Shin Yamaguchi.
I had thought that was the main station
For Yamaguchi City.

Turns out Shin means 'New' as in New Yamaguchi.
Not knowing that yet, once at Shin Yamaguchi,
I happily walked to buy a ticket for a local bus
To cross the central Japan mountains to Hagi.
This local bus is free by the way
If you hold the JR Pass.

It didn't go smoothly, even brandishing my pass.
Good fortune though, and a phone call from the ticket office
Swiftly brought running a very good English speaker
From Shin Yamaguchi Tourist Information Office.
As has always been the case, the enthusiasm is immense.
She explained that this wasn't the right station at all,
Walking me back up the stairs to platform 1
Where a little red train was waiting, the 11.12 to Yamaguchi City.

My host in Hagi, was expecting to meet me at half past four.
We had messaged via the Airbnb app the night before.
By the time the red train had got me to the right station,
I still had just under three hours to explore Yamaguchi City.
And I just loved it!
A famous red and five-storied pagoda was 1.4 kilometres away.
A simple walk, but I needed some coffee!
What seemed like a main street was a bit disappointing
So, I checked on the app, it said no problem, a café 2 minutes away.

Well, what did I walk into, but a beautiful glass roofed arcade.
The atmosphere was calm, people just happy with shopping to do.
A so dignified shop selling traditional sweets,
Packaged like precious diamonds, I ordered six.
All along the walls, certificates of excellence
Seemed hundreds of years old.

Fresh oysters in a basin with a fresh flowing tap
Ready to be cooked right there and eaten on the spot,
I'm sure that's what the sign said.

Before that, a whole shop with material for kimonos.
The fully dressed mannequins perfectly robed.
Inside, through the open door,
Customers were choosing their cloths.
I looked it up,
It's a five-year training, to become a kimono maker.

The coffee shop was a café and bar,
I sat inside and learned how to say *'mo ippai'*.
That just means, *another one please,*
Though it took a huddle of three baristas
With their phones searching dictionaries
As I haplessly gave up trying,
Before one of them shouted triumphantly,
"Wakatta! He means seconds! We got it!"

A serious department store drew me into its food hall.
The quality of the food! The way it was presented!
I wanted to go to stall after stall,
Fill basket after basket.
A cooked chicken salad for that evening's dinner
Proved delicious.

The arcade didn't have the push and the shove
You would expect on a Saturday.
There was room for everyone, I really liked that.
It was a gentle coming down, after Hiroshima.
In the family text I sent that evening
I said there was even a charity shop to explore.
A reply came back, *"Ooooh, a Japanese charity shop.*
Would love a rummage in there."

And now I'm in Hagi, by The Sea of Japan,
My JR bus trip across the 1,300m climb completed.
Out of the window were pine trees and occasional rice fields.
Along the side of one of those, a woman walked
Wearing wellingtons and a hat,
A hoe resting, work done, on her shoulder.

Toshiko san met me, concerned, the bus a little late.
The warmth of her welcome unconditional.
She stopped the car on the way to her home
To show me her town from a viewing point.
Seven islands, two rivers,
We shared a few thoughts.
Creating reassurance, like a belonging.

Her husband's name is Naoki san.
Their home is exquisite.

山口を楽しむ

2022年11月12日

　広島から南西に100キロほど離れた山口。当初は訪れる予定ではありませんでした。その時私は、中国山地を越えるバスに乗り換えようとしていました。電車の駅から出て、バス停まで歩き、そこで待つだけの予定でした。山口から日本海に面した萩までローカルバスに乗るのです。ゆっくり走るバスから、山をこえ村を抜け、景色を眺めようと思っていました。

　でも、電車の駅を間違えたために、山口にあるショッピング・アーケード"商店街"をうろつく素晴らしい日となったのでした。

　この後も、萩や姫路で2つのアーケード商店街に出会います。昔ながらのショッピング・アーケードは、それぞれに独自の名産品や雰囲気、個性があり、とても魅力的です。私は長く続くガラス屋根の下で、山口の商店街の古き良き店や人々に、感嘆し、楽しみ、素敵な数時間を過ごしました。

　この詩は、まず日本で過ごした日々がもたらした幸運を讃えます。その幸運は、この旅行のために貯め、銀行から借りたお金よりも、ずっと大きな価値がありました。

　広島駅で、私は知る限りのわずかな日本語で、なんとか山口までの新幹線の座席を予約することに成功しました。そして新山口駅では、萩までの行き方を教えてくれる素晴らしい人たちの惜しみなき寛大さに出会いました！

山口を楽しむ

出国前に銀行から
ありったけの金を引き出した
何の迷いもなく
でも幸運に恵まれた
日本に来てからの日々は
円換算レートをはるかに上回る価値があった

今日は、日本語で"キョウ"！
駅の窓口で「キョウ」と言えた

魔法の28日間ジャパンレールパスを手に
瞬く間に10：35発の新幹線に乗車
行き先は新山口
それが山口の
メインの駅だと思っていた

"シン"とは"新しい"という意味だった
そうとは知らず、新山口に到着
路線バスの券を買うために歩く
中国山地を越えて萩まで行くバスだ
ジャパンレールパスさえあれば
無料で乗れるバス

しかし私がパスを誇示しても、思い通りにはならなかった
窓口の担当者が電話すると
流暢な英語を話す人が走ってきてくれた
新山口観光局の人
いつものことながら、心のこもった対応
私は全く違う駅にいると教えてくれた
1番線のプラットホームの階段まで連れて行ってもらうと
11時12分発山口行きの、小さな赤い電車が待っていた

萩の宿に到着予定は4時半
前夜Airbnbのアプリにもメッセージを残した
赤い電車が正しい駅に連れて行ってくれると
まだ3時間弱ほど山口市を散策する余裕があった
最高だった！
有名な赤い五重塔は1.4キロ先
軽い散歩だが、コーヒーが飲みたかった
目抜き通りらしき道には少しがっかりした
でもアプリによると、問題ない、2分先にカフェがある

行き着いたのは、美しいガラスの屋根のアーケード
穏やかな雰囲気で、人々は買物を楽しんでいる。
堂々たる店構えの、伝統的な菓子屋
貴重なダイヤのような包みを6つ買った
壁に貼られた賞状は
何百年も前のもののようだ

新鮮な流水の中の、生きた牡蠣
その場で調理し食べる
多分、看板にそう書かれている

着物の生地に溢れる店
完璧な着付けのマネキン
開いた戸口から中を見ると
客が生地を選んでいる
調べたところ
和裁士になるには5年の修行が必要だ

カフェとバーのある店で
席について日本語で言う
"モウ　イッパイ"
バリスタが3人がかりで
携帯の辞書で調べている
私が諦めかけた時
ひとりが嬉しそうに叫んだ
「わかった！おかわりだ！了解！」

格式ある百貨店の食料品売場に引き寄せられる
その品質の高さ！陳列の素晴らしさ！
次々とカウンターに行き
カゴに入れまくりたくなる
その日の夕食のチキンサラダは
実に美味しかった

土曜日でも商店街は
ごった返してはいない
誰もがゆったりできる空間が、心地よかった
広島の後の気持ちの高ぶりが、優しく鎮まっていく
その晩、家族に送ったメッセージに
リサイクルショップもあった、と書いた
返答は、
「うわああ、日本のリサイクルショップ！」
「漁りたい！」

日本海に面した萩に到着
標高1300メートルを越えるバスの旅
窓からは、松の木や、時に水田が見えた
田んぼの脇を歩く女性
長靴と帽子姿で
ひと仕事終え、鍬を肩に担いでいる

待ち合わせたトシコさんは
バスが少し遅れたので心配そう
心からの、暖かい歓迎
お宅に向かう途中で車を止めて
萩の街の展望を見せてくれた
7つの島、2本の川
お互いの想いを少し述べあうだけで
信頼と結びつき

夫はナオキさん
とても素敵なお宅

HAGI ONE

Across The Generations
2022-11-13

I had a long time to plan my trip to Japan – as Covid-19 happened and a different journey emerged. A decision to search Airbnb for a long stay in a family home had revealed the home of Yoshiko san and Naoki san in Hagi. Yoshiko san spoke English and as a later poem reveals, was the most beautiful of hosts.

I had chosen Hagi as it was as close as I found to the coastal town of Senzaki, where the poet Kaneko Misuzu's museum was located.

This first poem from Hagi is an account of a visit to a major temple and historical location which held the story of Yoshida Shoin, one of Japan's mid-19th century modernising figures. The calm and the considered situation of this temple was opening my awareness more and more to the beauty of Japan.

There is the deepest beauty in an old couple holding hands. Such a couple offers the most powerful prompt to love. The children later in the poem are still bustling with what is yet to be and where future good fortune obliges acknowledgement.

Across The Generations

I watched in pleasure
The older couple holding hands,
Separating to read the signs on either side
Of the temple's tree lined path.
Once read, rejoining hands,
Moving together deliberately again.

The path held them to their stroll
Finding its way through the grounds
Of a Zen Buddhist temple called Tokoji.
Along its length, it is lined with trees
Each one with its own words of wisdom
Inscribed on an upright white plaque,
In a timeless corridor of learning.

They come from the writings of Yoshida Shoin
In 1859, and at age 29, executed for encouraging rebellion.
A quotation of his,

A mountain path, if often used, will quickly become a road.
If it is not used, it will soon become blocked up with sprouting grass and weeds.
This is so for the human heart too.

There seemed to be celebrations taking place.
Families gathered across the generations,
A photographer hired for the occasion.
At the centre of one, a young girl
Pleased and proud and wearing a kimono.
A boy, traditionally dressed, waited excitedly
By a stall selling sweet sticky dumplings on a stick.

Shichi-go-san is a festival every November 15th
When parents, visiting a shrine or a temple,
Celebrate the lives given to their children.
A prayer for health and prosperity
At ages *sichi* (seven), *go* (five) and *san* (three).

萩 1

世代を超えて
2022年11月13日

　日本の旅の計画は、随分と長い時間をかけました。コロナ禍が起き、別の旅もあり。Airbnbで見つけた長期滞在先の家庭が、萩にあるトシコさんとナオキさんの家だったのです。トシコさんは英語を話し、詩の中に書いたように、最高の宿主でした。

　萩を選んだ理由は、金子みすゞ記念館がある海辺の街、仙崎に近かったからです。

　萩で書いた最初の詩は、訪れた大きな寺や、19世紀半ばの日本の近代化の立役者、吉田松陰にゆかりある場所についてです。寺の落ち着いた思慮深い佇まいは、日本の美しさにますます目覚める体験となりました。

　その中でも最も深く美しかったのは、老カップルが手を繋ぐ姿でした。これほどにも愛に満ちたカップル。一方、詩の後半に登場する子供たちはこれからの希望に満ち、未来の幸せが願われています。

世代を超えて

楽しく眺める
老夫婦は繋いだ手を一旦離し
木々が立ち並ぶ寺への道の
両側の看板を読む
読み終えたら、また手を繋ぎ
一緒にゆっくりと歩いていく

ふたりが歩く小道は
寺の敷地を抜けて行く
禅宗の寺、東光寺
両側に立ち並ぶ樹々には
それぞれ智慧がこもっている
不朽の学びの道
白い立て看板に刻まれる

吉田松陰の書の言葉
1859年に、29歳にして、謀反を唱えたと処刑される
彼の言葉の引用だ

「山の小道というものは、
人が通っているうちは道ですが、
一度人が通らなくなると、
すぐに草が生え、塞がってしまうものです
人の心も同じ 」

お祝い事らしく
何世代もの家族が集まっていた
写真家も雇われていた
その中央に小さな女の子
嬉しそうな得意そうな着物姿
男の子も伝統的な装いで、ワクワクしながら待っている
傍らでは、甘い串団子を売っている

毎年11月15日は七五三
両親は、神社や寺を訪れ
子供たちに与えられた命を祝う
健康と繁栄を祈る
七歳、五歳、三歳の年に

HAGI TWO

Walking in Hagi
2022-11-(13-17)

I spent six days in Hagi, staying in Toshiko san and Naoki san's beautiful, traditional Japanese home. I spent one of those days with them showing me some of the town's most important landmarks and being taken into the mountain area. The other days I simply walked and found my way from one place to another – on one evening getting quite wet for the only time in Japan as I became a bit confused with the way back in the dark!

The old part of Hagi is of streets of wooden houses, formerly owned by the richer merchants and now beautifully preserved. There were even fresh flowers in a men's public loo! Twice I sat in the same old cafe, spoiled by its calm and comfort before walking out again.

In Hagi, I was at my most detached, interested to understand the transformation in Japan's late 19th century to the powerful industrial and militarised society it was to become just 50 years later. A local museum detailed the significance of Hagi as an early centre to those changes.

And of course, Hagi too had its covered *shōtengai* shopping arcade. I had the amazing good fortune of discovering it as a local music festival was happening inside. Rows of chairs were set up in the space in front of a community centre with a few food stalls and its traders association looking to bring in fresh customers.

I had some pieces of tonkatsu – Japanese fried pork – as I listened to the performers.

Hagi's *shōtengai* was struggling to survive, so causing my more anxious reflection on change.

Walking in Hagi

So much that is the history of Japan,
Walking in Hagi.
The Old Town Centre with its Edo period buildings,
The 265-year rule of the Shogunate and its Samurai
Eclipsed in fifty years by an Imperial restoration.
The Meiji modernisation, 1868 to 1912,
Industrialising, democratising,
Resisting colonialism from the West.

I walk for miles, the local museum a welcome rest.
My head filled with Meiji merchants' still perfect houses,
Light and shadows, screens and spaces,
Astonishing colours in exquisite gardens.
Textures that cause you to close your eyes,
To touch as if invisible, bowing to every corner,
Feeling all of this in all of my senses.
Hagiyaki, Hagi's pottery, laid out in studio after studio.

My first steps into the town were on a Sunday,
Encountering love enduring in a temple,
Families celebrating their children.
Otherwise, it was quiet, the centre at rest,
Until that is, I heard the sound of live music!
I followed, expecting a cafe in the open,
Instead, I turned into a real festival
Playing out the afternoon in Hagi's Tamachi Arcade.

Bizarrely, a line of Porsches sat one after the other
Sweeping down the narrow arcade
In a display of devil may care! We're here!
The poster said:
Porsche Fight Club Japan Choshu Domain!
On either side, enthusiasts admired and peered.
I went straight to the music,
Live Music for a Porsche, any day!

Some hours later, I had been entertained,
Had eaten tonkatsu fried pork from a family stall,
Bought some very large oranges for dinner later on.
The occasion, The Autumn Furusato Festival,
Furusato meaning hometown, as in Hagi!
A band, Summer Oranges, playing soft music and cool songs.
A night club's jazz singer and her trio, PKE Favorite,
A medley of covers, inoffensive, their name Quiche!
A local tartan-skirted teen pop idol, Saki Akiyama,
Heavy metal unbelievers, Aqua GeeCharn,
A young woman their leader, bassist, and singer.

As a fond farewell before I left,
I revisit the Tamachi arcade in the late afternoon.
It is empty, a jazz tune blowing down its length
Betraying the loneliness of a once loved
Best friend, left wondering how habits change
As shopping moves out of town and online.
A group of pensioners are being taught in a class,
Quite a few sat in rows, a young man out of place,
A tutor, pointing to a board explaining what to do.
The shop window I watched them through
Now a welfare centre of sorts.
The sign above the door, nuanced, once a music store!

Perhaps the energy of the cars on the first day,
The vibrancy of the musicians, the togetherness
Of the autumn festival will hold onto this space.
I want it to stay.

萩　2

萩の散策
2022年11月13日から17日

　私は萩のトシコさんとナオキさんの美しい日本の伝統に溢れるお宅に、6日間滞在しました。そのうち1日はおふたりと一緒に過ごし、街の大きな見所を案内してもらい、山に連れて行ってもらいました。その他の日は、私は1人であちらこちらと歩き回っていました。ある晩は暗くなって戻るのにちょっと迷ってしまい、日本滞在中に初めて、かなり雨に濡れてしまいました。

　萩の旧市街は、通りに木造の家が並び、かつての裕福な商人の家並みが美しく保存されています。男性用公衆トイレにも生花が飾られていました！　私は、昔ながらの同じ喫茶店を2度訪れ、落ち着いた居心地の良さを楽しみ、休み、また歩きました。

　萩では感情的になることなく、19世紀後期の日本の変貌に関心を持ちました。日本はわずか50年で産業化を果たし、軍国主義になっていったのでした。その変化の初期に萩が重要な役割を担ったことは、地元の博物館に詳しく展示されていました。

　そしてもちろん、萩にも屋根のついたアーケード、商店街がありました。しかも地元の音楽祭が開催されているという、驚くべき幸運に恵まれました。公民館の前のスペースに椅子が並べられて、食べ物の屋台がいくつか出ていて、客寄せをしていました。

　私はトンカツを食べ、演奏を聞きました。

　萩の商店街は、かなり苦戦しており、今後の変化がますます心配になりました。

萩の散策

日本の歴史に満ちた
萩の散策
旧市街中心部は江戸時代の建物
265年間に渡る、将軍と侍に支配された時代
王政復古によって50年ほどで勢いが陰る
1868年から1912年までの明治の近代化
産業化、民主化
西洋の植民地化への抵抗

長く歩いた後、地元の博物館で一息つく
明治時代の商人の、完璧に保存された家
光と影、障子や空間
見事な庭園の鮮やかな色彩
思わず目をつぶるような触感
見えないもののように触れ
隅々まで敬意を払って
五感のすべてで感じとる
次々と窯元に萩焼が並ぶ

初めて街に出たのは日曜日
寺では永続的な愛の姿に出会い
家族連れが子供の祝い事で賑わう
それ以外は静かで、休む街
でも急に生演奏の音楽が聞こえた！
屋外カフェかと行ってみると
本物の音楽祭だった
昼下がりの萩・田町商店街に演奏が流れる

奇妙なことに、たくさんのポルシェが並び
狭いアーケードを通っていく
どうだ！ この姿！
ポスターによると、
「ポルシェファイトクラブジャパン長州藩！」
両側には熱狂的なファンが集まる
私は音楽の方へまっしぐら
どんな時も、ポルシェより生演奏だ！

数時間音楽を楽しんだ後、
家族経営の店でトンカツを食べ
夕食用に大きなオレンジを買う
秋のふるさと祭り
ふるさとは、萩だ
サマー・オレンジーズという楽団が
ソフトでクールな曲を奏でる
ナイトクラブのジャズシンガーとPKE Favoriteトリオ
無難なカバーバンドの名前はキッシュ
タータン柄のスカートを履いた地元出身のティーンポップアイドル
秋山紗希
ヘビー・メタルと逆のAqua GeeCharn
バンドリーダーは、ベーシストかつシンガーの若い女性

去るのが名残惜しくて
午後遅くに、田町商店街を再訪する
人気はなく、ジャズが吹き抜ける
かつては愛された者の孤独
習慣が変わり、取り残された親友
街を離れて買物はオンラインに
年金受給者向けのクラスか
かなりの人が座っている中で
場違いに若い男性教師がボードを指しながら説明している
窓越しに覗いた店は
今は福祉センターなのか
入口の看板によると
かつては楽器屋だったらしい

最初の日に見た車のパレードの威勢の良さや
ミュージシャンの熱気
人々の連帯感など
秋祭りで見た活力が、この場所を支えてくれるかもしれない
そのまま残って欲しいと願う

HAGI THREE

Six Days in Hagi
2022-11-18

These six days in Hagi were the most complete six days I need ever have. In Toshiko san and Naoki san's traditional-styled Japanese home, I was given the gentlest of hospitality and the warmest of welcomes. There was no fuss, a simple acceptance of my being their guest having arrived to be in their home for a little while to be with a Japanese family.

Toshiko had been an English teacher and spoke with me very easily.

The part of their home given to the guest was of a traditional Japanese style, causing me to gasp with pleasure as I arrived on the first evening. Though traditional, it wasn't formal and sparse, offering as well, an ordinary homely and personal aesthetic. Falling asleep and waking up on the futon in the wooden screened room by their garden was to receive a gift that wove its way each day through all of my body and mind.

One evening I was invited to share the preparation of the locally harvested yuzu fruit to make an essential oil in Toshiko and Naoki's kitchen. Sacks of yuzu fruit had been brought in by their son Hiroki san and partner Noriko san. Noriko spoke fluent English and brought her friend and her friend's son, both of whom were learning English, so they could have some fun with me!

Hiroki san gave me a small jar of yuzu marmalade at the end of the evening. I am a marmalade lover – it was delicious over the next few days that it lasted.

One day, in the morning, Toshiko and Naoki took me out in their car to visit Hagi's historic landmarks. This included an experimental and Western style reverberatory furnace used in Hagi's 19th century industrial production. As well, they took me into Mt Kasayama's camellia grove – one day I shall go back in the spring to see those 25,000 camellia trees in their full red bloom! Naoki's sister-in-law, Midori san, joined us as we went to the underground caves – together, she and I sang Beatles' songs as we walked along to the caves' entrance!

On another day, Yoshiko returned wearing her full kimono from a tea ceremony class. She invited me to sit and drink a cup of matcha tea, ceremoniously served.

This poem is a thank you to Yoshiko san and to Naoki san for their unconditional kindness and beautiful living.

Six Days in Hagi

Sunshine radiates through the glass sliding doors.
It warms my body.
This corner of their home, still green leaves scintillating on trees
Lies in front of me.
It is Toshiko and Naoki san's garden,
It warms my very centre, my soul.

I am sat on the sofa. A low table
Has a white cloth, scenes of temples
Embroidered, as though I needed reminding
Of where I am. I close my eyes,
I open them again, I am in Hagi,
Yamaguchi Prefecture, Japan.

The garden and the high hills rise to a cloudless sky,
I look out and breathe the colours in.
This is part only of what I take with me
When at 13.16 I catch a bus to Tsuwano.
I am sad.

I want to remember these names.
Midori, Hiroki, Noriko, Naoki, Toshiko.
I want to remember Yuzu marmalade,
A little jar given to me by Toshiko's son,
The remains eaten this morning, spoonfuls
Adding its tang to my bananas and yoghurt.

Six days in this beautiful home,
The entrance opening to a curved wooden step.
Leaving my shoes, I walked into the signs and symbols
Of a Japanese aesthetic, ornaments, and an oil painting.
A pencilled drawing of a mountain scene and a pagoda,
An old-fashioned lamp on top of a piano,
A music sheet for Chopin's music waiting.

Turn left, turn right, or straight ahead,
Wooden polished floors,
Sliding door upon sliding door.

I slept on the futon, in the eight-tatami mat room.
The alcove complete with a geisha doll,
The perfectly placed flowers in their white vase.
Toshiko's own scroll, hanging ceiling to floor,
Her calligraphy as a girl winning a national prize.
In the morning the light greeted my opening eyes
The screens facing the garden left open.
The day began with a calmness of mind
The entire surroundings, the textures, the sounds,
The natural and the created beauty, briefly mine.

It's tempting to recount the places they took me to.
So, I will ...
Mt Kasayama, a volcano and a peninsula
Looks out to seven islands in The Sea of Japan.
On two of those, Naoki and Yoshiko's parents were born.
Yoshiko remembers a twice-yearly boat trip as a child
She didn't take to the waves, like me, easily seasick.
We went down steps to the inside of the crater
Though shallow the volcanic rock intimidated.
Not so to Naoki, a scholar and a geographer.

At the base of the mount is a camellia grove,
A few months early to see the flowers,
They blossom in a vast blanket of red.
Trees in their thousands, there because once it was thought
That to walk in their direction
Was to venture through a demon's gate,
Going there forbidden, the trees were protected.
We climbed a tall tower, black kites circling overhead,
My imagination desperate to see the trees in blossom.

The kites, by the way, gather by the dozen
Swooping down on unwitting tourists
Leaving them screaming and no longer with their sandwich.
I saw them by a café, flying down far too low
I couldn't count there were so many.

The earliest remnants of Japan's industrial revolution
Include important sites in Hagi.
There is a reverberatory furnace and the Ebisugahana shipyard.
We walked around both of these before eating
In a quick stop and go lunch time meal place.
A perfect bowl of soba noodles with wakame,
Workers coming in and out, orders rapidly put through.

From there we went to Midori san's home,
A 350-year-old building wrapped in a densely packed garden,
The house itself seeming miraculously still standing.
Midori, is married to Naoki's brother
Her name expresses the green of the leaves and the plants.
She served us her green tea in small bowls,
Offered me a gorgeous crafted pink cake
Sat on the floor, a little discomfort irrelevant.

I had innocently said, the underground caves,
When Toshiko had asked, was there anywhere else?
I hadn't known they were a good drive away,
But it didn't quell the excitement, it had been a while.
Naoki had earlier picked, and held in his hand
A long sturdy stem of pampas grass.
Now we encountered whole hillsides shimmering like glass
As the sun reflected upon masses of their long blond hair.

The limestone cave, Akiyoshi-do, lies within a Quasi National Park,
One of the largest in Japan, it is 100 metres underground.
We walked through a small town to access the entrance
It's good days of busy shops long gone in a pre 21st century past.
It's not cold as the temperature stays steady,
A comfortable walk encountering the waterworn rocks and stalactites.
Midori had stayed back, her hip recently replaced.

It was falling dark as we reached a mountain top observatory
Just late enough for the café to be closing,
Enough light left, to climb the viewing point
To scan the wide horizon of Akiyoshidai Plateau
To take photos, to remember being together
A smile for the camera, the four of us happy.

On the way to the restaurant, Midori checked in at home
She came back with a bag of small oranges and two pomegranates.
They are for you, from my husband, she said!

The restaurant was a practical conclusion to a long day.
More pleasure as well which we all welcomed.
The question to me was what kind of dining?
Japanese of course, and if possible, ni-sakana, I said.
Ni-sakana is a simmered white fish, a favourite of Naoki's.
That being the case, where to eat chose itself,
A local fish restaurant, wooden raised benches,
A small bottle of the local sake,
Being hungry I asked for a tofu dish as well.
The whole day remarkable.

I'm finishing this poem in Tsuwano
High in the hills, the Hoshi Ryokan
Where I am staying.
I am lonely for the first time in Japan
Missing the home I was given,
Six days in Hagi.

萩　3

萩の6日間
2022年11月18日

　萩での6日間は、これまでで最も充実した6日間でした。トシコさんとナオキさんの伝統的な和風の家で、最高に優しいもてなしを受け、暖かく歓迎されました。大騒ぎするわけではなく、訪れた私の存在を、日本の家庭にすんなりと受け入れてくれたのです。

　トシコさんは英語教師だったので、私とも気楽に話ができました。

　来客が泊まるのは伝統的な日本家屋で、私は到着した最初の晩に、嬉しくて息を呑みました。伝統的であっても、堅苦しさやよそよそしさはなく、普通の家庭的な雰囲気で、その人柄が満溢れていました。庭に面した障子張りの部屋の布団で眠り目覚めるのは、私の体や心に染み渡る贈物のような日々でした。

　ある晩、地元で収穫した柚子をエッセンシャルオイルにするからと、トシコさんとナオキさんの台所に招かれました。柚子の袋を持ってきたのは、息子のヒロキさんとパートナーのノリコさんでした。ノリコさんは英語に堪能で、また一緒に来た友人と息子さんは英語を学んでいるので、私と一緒に楽しもうと言うのです！

　その晩の終わりに、ヒロキさんは、柚子のマーマレードの小瓶をくれました。私はマーマレードが大好きなので、数日のうちに美味しく頂いてしまいました。

　ある朝トシコさんとナオキさんは、車で萩の史跡へと連れて行ってくれました。その中には、19世紀の産業化時代に使われた、実験的な西洋風の反射炉もありました。また笠山椿群生林にも連れて行ってもらいました。いつか春に訪れて、2万5千本の椿の赤い花が満開のところを見たいものです！　ナオキさんの義理の妹のミドリさんも合流して、地下の洞穴の入口まで、一緒にビートルズを歌っていきました！

　別の日には、トシコさんが着物姿で、茶道のお稽古から帰ってきました。私も誘われて、厳かに出される抹茶をいただきました。

　これは、トシコさんとナオキさんの惜しみない優しさと美しい暮らしに感謝を捧げる詩です。

萩の6日間

引き戸のガラスを通して陽の光が輝き
私の体を温める
ここでは、まだ木々の緑の葉が生き生きときらめく
私の目の前にあるのは
トシコさんとナオキさんの庭
私の中心、魂を温めてくれる存在

ソファに座る。低いテーブルには
白い布に寺の風景の刺繍
どこにいるか想い出させるためか
目を閉じて
また開けても、萩にいる
日本の山口県の萩

庭と、雲ひとつない空へそびえる高い丘
外を見ながら、色彩を吸い込む
せめてそれだけでも持って帰ろう
13時16分には津和野行きのバスが出る
悲しい

ずっと名前を覚えていたい
ミドリ、ヒロキ、ノリコ、ナオキ、トシコ
柚子のマーマレードも忘れない
トシコさんの息子がくれた小瓶
今朝、最後の一口を食べた
バナナとヨーグルトに酸味を加えて

美しい家での6日間
玄関を入ると木製の段があり
そこに靴を置いて、中に入る
美しい和風の、飾りや油絵
山の景色や五重の塔の鉛筆画が飾られ
ピアノの上には旧式の照明
ショパンの楽譜が待っている
左へ、右へ、まっすぐ
磨かれた板の間
引き戸、そしてまた引き戸

8畳間の布団で眠った
床の間には舞妓人形
白い花瓶に完璧に活けられた花
トシコさんの書いた掛け軸が
天井から床まで下がっている
娘時代に書道の全国大会で賞をとった時のもの
朝、目を開けると光が迎える
庭に面した引き戸は開けっ放し
心穏やかに1日が始まる
周囲のすべて、手触りも、音も
自然や物の美しさが、すべて束の間私のもの

一緒に行った場所を思い出したい
そう……
笠山、火山と半島
日本海の七つの島を眺めたこと
ナオキさんとトシコさんのご両親が生まれた2つの島もある
トシコさんは子供の頃、年に2度船で渡ったそうだ
私と違って、波で船酔いはしない
階段を降りて火口に入った
深くはないが、そそり立つ溶岩は威圧的
だが、博識な地理学者のナオキさんは気にしない

山の麓の椿の群生林
数ヶ月早ければ花盛りで
大きな赤い毛布のように咲いていた
ここに何千本もの樹々があるのは
この方向に歩くのは
鬼門だとされたからだ
立入禁止だったから、樹々は守られた
高い展望台に登ると、黒いタカが頭上を旋回した
どうしても樹々が花咲くところが見たい

ところで、タカは12羽ほど集まっていた
気づかぬ観光客に急降下して
叫んでももう遅く、サンドイッチはない
喫茶店の近くでも、ずっと低空飛行
あまりにも多くて数えきれない

日本の産業化初期の名残
萩の名所でもある
反射炉と恵美須ヶ鼻造船所跡
食事の前に歩いて回った
その後、食事処で短い休憩
完璧なワカメ蕎麦
仕事の合間の人たちが出入りし、注文は迅速だ

ミドリさんの家に行く
350年前の建物は、ぎっしり生い茂る庭に包まれる
まだあることが奇跡のような家
ミドリさんは、ナオキさんの弟と結婚した
葉や植物の緑を表す名前
小さな器に緑茶を注ぎ
手の込んだ桃色の美しいお菓子を出してくれる
床に座る居心地の悪さも気にならない

トシコさんがどこに行きたいかと聞いた時
洞穴に行きたいと、無邪気に言ったけど、
こんなに離れた場所とは知らなかった
でも、しばらくたっても、興奮は抑えられない
ナオキさんが摘んだのは
長く頑丈なシロガネヨシの茎
丘の斜面全体が、草のようにそよいでいる
太陽が反射する、大量の長い金髪

秋吉台国定公園の、石灰岩の鍾乳洞
日本でも最大級で、地下100メートルにある
小さな街を通り抜けて、入口へと向かう
店が賑わったのも遠い昔、21世紀以前のことだ
気温は安定し、それほど寒くはなく
気持ちよく散歩していると、水で磨耗した岩や鍾乳石が現れる
最近股関節の手術をしたミドリさんは、先には行かない

頂上の展望台についた時には暗くなり始めていた
喫茶店は閉店してしまった
展望台まで登るだけの明るさはある
秋吉台の広い水平線を見渡し
一緒に過ごした思い出の写真撮影
カメラに向かって微笑む、幸せな4人

食事に向かう途中で、ミドリさんは家に寄って
小さなオレンジとザクロが2つ入った袋を手に戻る
夫からあなたに、と渡される

長い一日の後、外食は合理的だ
全員がもてなしを受けて、楽しめる
どんな料理がいいかと聞かれる
もちろん和食、できたら煮魚
白身魚の煮魚は、ナオキさんの好物
それなら、行く場所は決まった
地元の魚料理屋、木製のベンチ
地元の酒の小瓶
お腹が空いたので、豆腐も頼んだ
丸一日素晴らしかった

津和野でこの詩を書き上げる
高い丘の上の星旅館
今はここに泊まる
日本に来て、初めてさみしくなる
あの家が恋しい
萩の6日間が

SENZAKI

Kaneko Misuzu Museum
2022-11-15

Kaneko Misuzu was a Japanese poet in the early years of the 20th century. Her home was Senzaki, a small fishing village on the coast of the Sea of Japan. I came across her poetry published in a really beautiful American hardback edition titled: Are You an Echo? The Lost Poetry of Misuzu Kaneko.

Brought to print by David Jacobson, this unusual bilingual book translated by Sally Ito and Michiko Tsuboi 'tells the story of the poet's life alongside some of her most beloved poems, illustrated in tender watercolour by Japanese artist, Toshikado Hajiri.'

I then found all of her poems in English and collected in four volumes by Mayumi Itoh. I took one of those books in my backpack to Japan and left it with Toshiko san.

I had discovered Kaneko Misuzu's poems and her story not long before starting my language lessons with Lisa sensei. The main part of the following 40 odd weeks of lessons we spent reading and discussing the poems, whilst I practised speaking Japanese by reading them out loud.

And so, visiting the Kaneko Misuzu Memorial Museum in Senzaki became the central focus for my travel in Japan:

I came down from Hagi to Nagatoshi, which encompasses Senzaki, on a small train passing in and out of the coves and villages marking this part of the coast of the Sea of Japan. Again, I walked slowly around the quiet streets to reach the museum so as to somehow prepare, almost like a pilgrim, for my meeting with the poet.

Senzaki

The Kaneko Misuzu Museum

As usual, I walked from the station.
Having arrived in Nagatoshi, her town being Senzaki,
I took the 60 minutes to slowly absorb the sea,
Looking out to Benten Island, still there I hoped.
I was reluctant to arrive, wanting to linger,
Look at the wooden buildings, find myself
In an alleyway, a large cemetery, the memorials
Connected with Buddhism, the temple at the centre.

The museum isn't set apart,
Either side various shops,
Its situation very ordinary, not heroic.
I held back still, feeling sad, her story
Inseparable from her poems.
The entrance however is open to the street,
A child on a poster, hands by her side
Invites you into the wide-fronted building.

Immediately, you step into a bookstore
The original building where she worked and lived,
Brought from the port of Shimonoseki.
The bookstore has two floors,
On the ground, the pens, the shelves of books.
Steep stairs lead to the second,
To the lamps, the sets of drawers,
A paper flower in a vase.

Each glance of the eye slows down thought
These objects are ones that she walked past.
A pencil on a desk, by an open notebook,
Like one she would have held in her hand.
Everything that attaches each of us to the other
Is held in these items. The floor where I stand
Reverberating as my footsteps trace hers.

A small, gravelled courtyard has her statue,
Low to the ground, a stone engraved with a poem,
Not quite a shrine.
The path takes you to her poems and the story of her life.

The modern building has smooth, sliding glass doors
It's light inside and a corridor is where I later sat
Stamped the museums mark on 15 postcards.
Each one a different poem, its artwork revealing which.
Amongst them, of course, *Hoshi to Tanpopo,*
Stars and Dandelions.

I took Mayumi Itoh's book from my bag
To bridge the gap of communication.
The staff were delighted and gracious
That I should have travelled so far,
Selling me another book of poetry,
A dozen bookmarks and 48 postcards.

Her famous picture
Faces the entrance to an exhibition room.
Two sides, both walls, reveal an account
Of her birth to her death.
Alongside, glass cabinets hold the physical display.
A cabinet in the centre has a book
Its pages open.
I lacked a translation of the exhibit,
Felt it as the original poetry, as she wrote it.

Her poems are everywhere you look
Being read out loud in a corner with seats,
In the books for sale, all beautifully laid out.
The longer you linger, the more
They wrap her personality around you.

But it's the curved passageway with dimmed light
That, even without the translation, and
Just fragments of her poems in my head,
Causes you to lift your whole being
And give yourself to Kaneko Misuzu.
Spaced along either wall,
So the reader can walk up, then back,
Are her poems, each in a glass frame.
Coming from each is a light, below a few is a chair.
The instruction to the reader, sit down
And listen to the poem being read.
Take your time, listen, and listen again.

If next to a poem in its glass frame,
Two hands are held out together
Put your own out in front of you.
And there, written on your palms,
Or, on the back of your hands
A beam of light projects a poem.

I loved being there, those beautiful words
Which made me come to Japan.

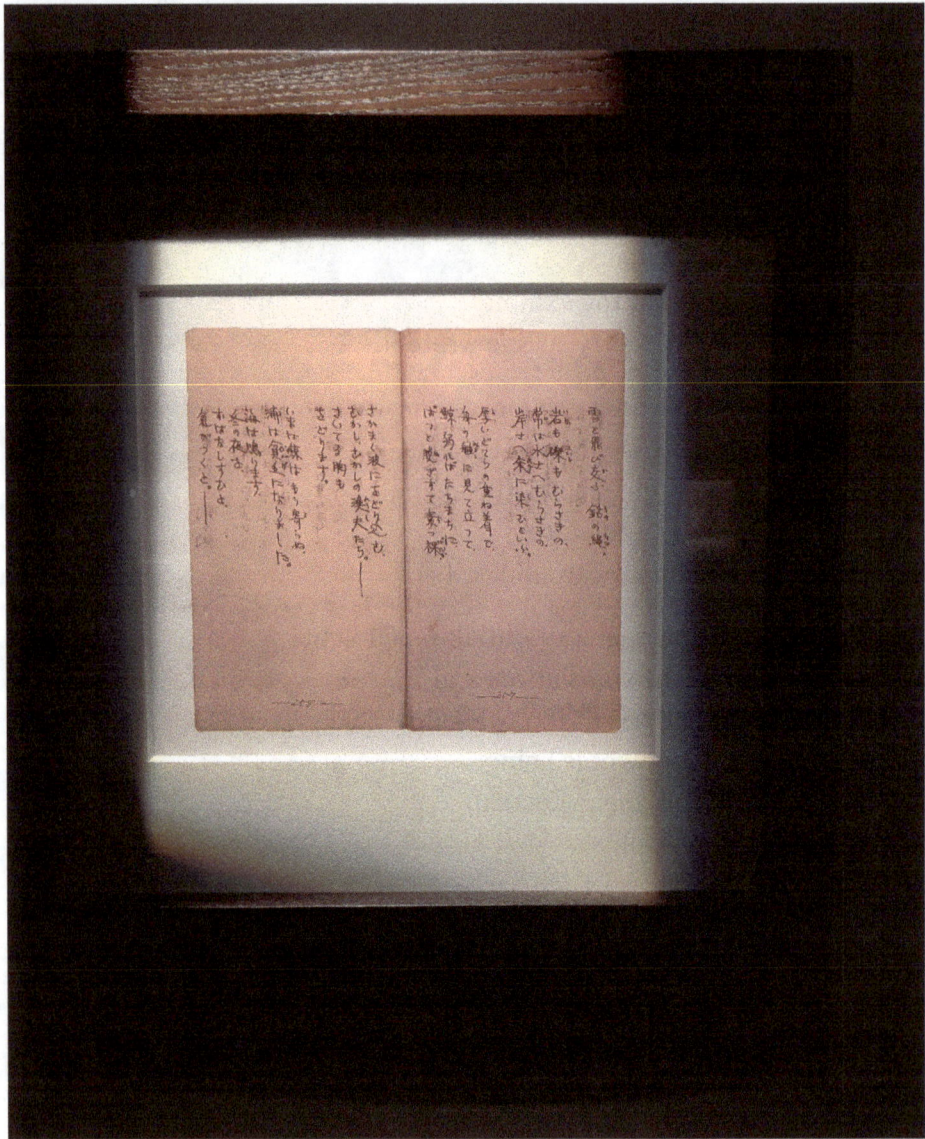

I had a dandelion tattooed on my left wrist, its stem reaching into my hand around 2010. It represented renewal and new life. On my return from Japan, I then had a star tattooed in mirror position on my right wrist and hand. This was so each time that I look at my hands I can see Kaneko Misuzu's poem *Hoshi to Tanpopo, Stars and Dandelions*, written there. Her poem too, speaks of renewal and new life.

Stars and Dandelions

Kaneko Misuzu

Deep in the blue sky,
like pebbles at the bottom of the sea,
lie the stars unseen in daylight
until night comes.
You can't see them, but they are there.
Unseen things are still there.

The withered, seedless dandelions
hidden in the cracks of the roof tile
wait silently for spring,
their strong roots unseen.
You can't see them, but they are there.
Unseen things are still there.

仙崎

金子みすゞ記念館
2022年11月15日

金子みすゞは、20世紀初めの日本の詩人です。故郷である仙崎は、日本海に面した小さな漁村です。私が彼女の詩に出会ったのは、アメリカで出版された美しいハードカバーの本、『こだまでしょうか？ いちどは失われた みすゞの詩』でした。

デイヴィッド・ジェイコブソンによる、珍しいバイリンガルの書籍で、翻訳はサリー・イトウと坪井美智子が手がけ、「詩人の生涯と、最も愛される詩のいくつかを、日本の画家羽尻利門の優しい水彩画で物語る」と記されています。

その後、マユミ・イトウによる英訳された詩をすべて収録した4部作を見つけました。そのうちの1冊をバックパックに入れて日本に持って行ったので、トシコさんにあげました。

私が金子みすゞの詩に出会ったのは、リサ先生の日本語レッスンを始める少し前でした。その後40数週間にわたるレッスンの大半を、詩を読み語り合い、音読して会話の練習をしました。

だから、仙崎にある金子みすゞ記念館を訪れるのは、私の日本の旅の目玉だったのです。

萩から仙崎のある長門市までは、日本海沿いの入江や村を巡る小さな電車で行きました。ここでもまた、ゆっくりと静かな通りを歩き回って、記念館へと向かいました。巡礼者のように、詩人に出会う心の準備をしたのです。

仙崎
金子みすゞ記念館

いつものように、駅から歩く
長門市に到着し、彼女の故郷の仙崎へ
ゆっくりと海を見ながら60分
弁天島が見えるといいなと思いながら
まだ着いてしまいたくない
うろうろしたいが
木造の家々を見ながら
小道に入り大きな墓地や記念碑のある所へ出る
仏教と縁深く、中央にはお寺

記念館は通り沿いで
両側にはいろいろな店があり
普通の佇まい、英雄気取りではない
でも悲しいのは、彼女の身の上
詩とは切っても切れない
入口は外へと開かれている
ポスターに描かれた子供が、手は傍に
間口の広い建物へと誘っている

入ると、すぐに書店
彼女が育った書店が
生家跡に復元されたもの
書店は2階建て
1階にはペンや書棚があり
急な階段を上ると2階
ランプ、引き出し
花瓶の中の紙の花

何か見るたびに想いにひたる
かつて彼女が、その傍を歩いたもの
机には開いたままのノートの横に
彼女が手に握ったであろう鉛筆
これらの品にこめられた想いが人々を結び付ける
私が立つ床も
足音が彼女の足音とこだまする

小さな砂利敷きの中庭に、彼女の像
地面には、詩を刻んだ石碑
祀るわけではない
彼女の詩と人生の物語へ誘う小道

近代的な建物、滑らかなガラスの引き戸
室内は明るく、後にそこに腰掛ける廊下
記念館のスタンプが押された15枚のハガキ
各々に異なる詩と、ちなんだ絵が描かれる
その中には、もちろん、
「星とたんぽぽ」もある

カバンからマユミ・イトウの本を取り出し
言葉が伝わらない時の橋渡し
スタッフは喜び
遠くから来た私に感謝する
購入したのは、もう1冊の詩集と
12枚のしおりと48枚のハガキ

彼女の有名な写真が
展示室の入口で迎える
両側の壁に展示されるのは
彼女の誕生から死までの歩み
ガラスの陳列台には、ゆかりの品が並ぶ
中央のキャビネットには1冊の本
ページは開いている
展示の説明は英訳がないけれど
おそらく彼女の自筆の詩

どこを見ても彼女の詩
隣の席で朗読され
販売される本は美しく陳列され
長くいればいるほど
その人柄に包まれる

薄明かりの曲がりくねる通路
英訳がなくてもわかる
詩の一節が頭に浮かぶだけで
自身のすべてが高揚し
金子みすゞに身を委ねる
壁に挟まれたスペースを
読者は行ったり来たり
ガラスの額に入った詩
それぞれ光に照らされ、
下にはいくつかの椅子
読者に座るよう促す
そして詩の朗読を聞くように
じっくりと、何度も

ガラスの額に入った詩の隣に
ふたつの手を差し出す印があれば
自分の手も差し出そう
その手のひらに
または手の甲に
光で詩が投射される

美しき言葉を満喫する
このために日本に来たのだから

　私の左手首から手のひらへと、タンポポの茎が伸びる刺青を入れたのは、2010年頃でした。それは新生と新たな命を表しています。日本から戻って、私は反対側の右手の同じ場所に、星の刺青を入れました。手を見るたびに、金子みすゞの『星とたんぽぽ』という詩が見えるのです。彼女の詩も、新生と新たな命を描いています。

星とたんぽぽ

金子みすゞ

青いお空のそこふかく、
海の小石のそのように
夜がくるまでしずんでる、
昼のお星はめにみえぬ。
見えぬけれどもあるんだよ、
見えぬものでもあるんだよ。

ちってすがれたたんぽぽの、
かわらのすきに、だァまって、
春のくるまでかくれてる、
つよいその根はめにみえぬ。
見えぬけれどもあるんだよ、
見えぬものでもあるんだよ。

TSUWANO ONE

Shamisen in Tsuwano
2022-11-19

I stood with Yoshiko san at the bus stop across the street from her house and we waited for me to get on the local bus to Tsuwano. I was reluctant to leave – the six days in Hagi and in Toshiko and Naoki's beautiful home had wrapped so perfectly around me.

Tsuwano though was up in the higher hills, and I was also looking forward to the promise of its old samurai mansions with white earthen walls, dark red roof tiles, and wooden grated windows lining the streets. I found those streets and walked along them in warm sun alongside channels of clear flowing water filled with colourful and mesmerising koi carp!

I stayed three nights in the Hoshi (Star) Ryokan (traditional inn) where for the second time, I indulged in Japanese kaiseki cuisine – exquisite food served all at once in beautiful bowls with local and seasonal produce.

On the first morning I was finishing my kaiseki breakfast and could hear the sound of traditional Japanese music. I walked outside and noticed a poster in the ryokan window. It was advertising a theatre, dance, and music festival happening that same day! The hostess had tried to explain about it at breakfast – but my Japanese hadn't been up to understanding what she had said.

I was astonished at my good luck – falling on my feet into multiple outdoor performances of traditional Japanese performing arts.

At the end of the day, I asked if I could have the poster – which the ryokan owner was very pleased to give me!

I walked to and from the two outdoor venues – one in the grounds of a temple for the Noh theatre and the other by the station for the dancing and music. A few small family stalls offered games and sweets to the children and various plates of hot food to the adults.

I was soothed and enthralled into the enjoyment of the music and dance and theatre which I had hoped to find – perhaps in Kyoto or in Tokyo in a commercial event. Yet here, in Tsuwano, I was given the most extraordinary local festival with the highest quality of performers – free.

A dance performance by older women wearing traditional kimonos continuously moving in a large circle is a memory I shall forever hold.

I had first heard the shamisen – a plucked three string instrument – as a young man while watching the films of the Japanese director, Akira Kurosawa. Ever since, I had listened to recordings and loved the sounds of traditional Japanese music – now I was listening to it in person.

Genji-maki is a recommended local specialty in Tsuwano. It is a kind of confectionery made with sweet bean paste rolled with thin sponge cake. Not too sweet and – as I found out – it goes very well with Japanese tea.

Shamisen in Tsuwano

Tsuwano held its Autumn Festival on the 19th of November,
In the open air, in front of the station,
Inside the gates of a temple,
Along the streets in shops and places tucked away
There were spaces with games for children to play.
Including a basin with a tricky handheld net
To chance your luck and come away with a goldfish!
There was a stall with grilled chestnuts,
Adults waiting their turn whilst the children waited for their sweets.

The guest house host had seen me going out
This time succeeding in telling me
That the flyer she had in her hand
Was the timetable of events and where they were happening.
She had tried as I had breakfast
But that was without the benefit of the clues
As the street invited me out.
It's as if they knew I was coming!

It was only 10am but already events had started.
I centred myself at the station,
Its front lined with tables of local craft and produce.
There were two performance venues,
The Taiko drummers were clear on the poster
Their time though not until 12:30.
I strolled into the town's main street
Where very soon there was the sound of a flute
I turned into the temple and stopped still, astonished.

The musicians sat white robed with black hats
While centre stage, Noh performers moved in stylised dance,
Clothed in rich gold brocade, this performance,
For the first part, unmasked.
The sideways flute cast its high pitch throughout,
A girl playing, it seemed the ensemble was a family,
The father singing and playing a drum,
The youngest, a boy, playing small cymbals.

It is demanding to watch not knowing the form,
The actors' extraordinarily precise movements
Obliging an informed and learned attention.
Much more so, was that the case,
When I returned for a second performance.
This time, the characters fearfully masked.
One more benign, the other definitely a demon.
Their robes were more ornate, more otherworldly,
A bow and two arrows held prominently.

Noriko san later told me the performance was *Kagura*,
A selfish god becoming a hero
Helping girls from the village escape from the Orochi,
A huge snake, in the finale defeated.

I found time for a coffee and three genji-maki
Sweet pastries, filled with bean paste,
These ones local to Tsuwano.
The festival was free, a performance space for everyone,
I couldn't believe my unplanned good fortune
When seated in front of the station, those
Muscled male physiques started their drumming.
Two flutes played by women pierced the air
Accompanying the thunder of those majestic drums.
As backdrop, the range of hills encircling the town

No sooner had the drummers turned their backs
When some 30 women, all seeming over 70,
Dressed in formal kimonos,
Appeared and created a circle, heads high,
Bodies in readiness to dance, beauty in movement.
The music was traditional Japanese song,
So precise hand and foot shapes.
Elegant flowing movements in a never-ending wave.
This perhaps was the moment in Japan I shall most remember.

A more raucous interpretation of dance followed
Enormous flags almost replacing the sky,
The emblems of the groups proudly choreographed.
One of them was a deep blue, an orange koi swimming.
More loosely dressed, these dancers were having fun
Leaping in and out of intricate patterns
Sometimes led by a singer, standing to the side.

Don't let me leave out the magician, a young man
Vaudeville-like performing, his tricks entertaining!

The festival ended with a shamisen player.
I'm sure she was celebrated, her playing
Like an extension of herself, the strings plucked
By a large pick, called a *bachi*.
Her voice, impeccably rising, folktales
I sensed, a long way back in time.
Accompanied by a second shamisen player
And a third with an arm held drum,
Holding a second with his leg on a number of songs.

I hadn't expected to hear the shamisen being played.
Music listened to for the first time
Watching a Kurosawa film in Edinburgh
A series on TV, some 50 years previously.

TSUWANO TWO

Three Girls and Their Umbrellas
2022-11-23

On the day after the autumn festival, I stepped out to walk down the old streets of Tsuwano. These were the wide streets lined by the houses of the wealthy merchants and samurai from the Edo period (1603 to 1868), and it was on one of those streets that I came upon three young girls with their open umbrellas.

I don't think I could have made a more perfect living sculpture of synchronised innocence and beauty when young children are with themselves alone and are creating sense of their immediately present lives.

Each one of these many extraordinary moments in Japan, alone justified my journey. The day before had been full of its sounds, scents and movement – this one small moment observing three children, its own unique jewel of contentment.

I climbed the steps to the Taikodani Shrine, nestled on a hillside 350m above the town. This offered the uniquely Japanese experience of walking through an ascending tunnel of some one thousand vermillion lacquered red gates, called torii. Being autumn, the many maple trees were shedding their red and orange leaves, laying an astonishing red leafed path under my feet as I climbed to the shrine.

From the height of the temple into the carpark below, I watched an inept father or grandfather struggling with managing a baby … reminding me of the ordinary as well as the divine!

The koi swimming in the clear and fast flowing streams in channels running along the side of the main Tono-machi Street were almost not believable. They have been swimming there since the Edo period.

Three Girls and Their Umbrellas

It was hardly rain, enough nonetheless
For these young girls to show off their umbrellas.
It can't have been coincidence, the designs so similar
Only best friends would have planned such togetherness.
Their place in the street, a photographer's dream.
They were talking as young children do,
Earnestly and happily, and shoulder to shoulder.
The colours, the pinks and the purple,
It was all I could do to keep myself
From running right up to them,
Please, where can I buy one!

Though slightly overcast, the day had been filled
With autumn, red vermilion, street canals full of koi,
Families out on a Sunday, more children in kimonos.
Even a very brand-new baby. I stared transfixed
As the dad had no clue how to transfer
From his arms to the car. It may have been grandad.
Mum was ah, let's see what he can do
I'm with the baby's big sister, who has my attention.
She did, in due course, sort the baby as well,
The dad, or was it grandad, released, lit up a cigarette.

I was standing by the wall of a shrine,
The shrine was huge, one of the five greatest in Japan.
Tsuwano's Taikodani shrine is dedicated to Inari,
The Shinto god of agriculture.
Statues and images of foxes adorn the grounds,
They are said to be Inari's messenger.
I gave 500 yen for a face mask of a fox,
Hung it in front of the shrine's main hall.
On the back, I wrote down the names of my children,
Their partners and their children,
So that the kami, the spirits, could receive my wishes
And give me their blessing.

Inside there was a celebrant, chanting prayers,
Moving in circles before the deity
Shaking a clutch of small bells in either hand,
A gold head dress and flowing robes, shamanistic.

A winding path leads up to the holy grounds,
One thousand red vermillion torii gates along its way.
On my walk through each one, I snapped
Photo upon photo, the autumn maple leaves falling
A red carpet of calm rolling beneath the red gates.

The koi really do swim in street canals
Fresh flowing water at the side of the houses.
These areas are preserved, reminding nonetheless
That once upon a time, when under siege,
These koi were the inhabitants' food.
Now they are large, mostly dark grey, but some white,
Classically reddish pink and black spotted, the form
Adorning Japanese art, swimming against the current,
Overcoming obstacles, success through perseverance.

It was by these canals that I came across the children
They were long past interested, local,
And on their way to somewhere much more important.
To one of their houses or, more likely,
Being the end of the afternoon, returning.

TSUWANO THREE

Inari's Mist
2022-11-21

This poem, written on the day I left Tsuwano, is a simple reflection on the temples and shrines I stepped into and walked past while travelling in Japan. I have no need personally for a supernatural explanation of what, why, and how things are. Yet the principles expressed in the Japanese relation between themselves and those places honouring deities, including in their own homes, brought to my experience a challenge to the disconnected singularity of my own living.

I felt more connected to people, to place, and to a common purpose when allowing these temples and shrines to give me a helping hand.

The Shinto deity, Inari, is venerated as the holy power of foxes, fertility, rice, tea and sake, of agriculture and industry.

Inari's Mist

The mountain mist, following overnight rain,
Sat gently just above the town. Inari's moisture,
Reaching to the rice fields with gratitude,
Replaced the morning sky as I left Tsuwano.

Tsuwano had been kind. Taking me by the hand
Into a dreamland of theatre, music, and dance.
The *Shichifukujin* are Japan's seven lucky gods.
Each one has surely been with me,
At every table I have sat and ate,
By every futon where I have slept.
Beside each and every person I have met.

It's not possible to travel the distances I have
Along coastlines, into mountains, and in its cities.
To be unaware of the constancy
Of Japanese observance of their temples and shrines.
They are magnificent and also, they are insignificant.
They are gold and vermillion red and also, they are worn,
Adorned only by a tree or a small bunch of flowers.

The intention is not to be oppressive, instead
Inviting consideration of our relationships
With the natural world we inhabit,
With the future of the planet,
How we are with each other.
They are religion and yet not,
Incompatible with being an atheist
But then in the Buddhist and Shinto tradition
There is no creator God.

I enjoyed the easy way people came and went
A candle lit, a stick of incense left burning,
Or a simple bow of the head.
An acknowledgement of our interdependent place
Our vulnerability without the other.

HIMEJI ONE

2022-11-24

Himeji is most famous for its glorious castle. I stayed in a room in a shared flat above a kimono shop in the centre of its amazing *shōtengai, or* covered arcade. This poem is about being in the exquisite gardens of the castle and coming across a young girl, her mother, and grandmother.

The three generations had come into the gardens to photograph the girl – I am assuming connected to the age of five and the recent *shichi-go-san* (seven-five-three) festival when parents celebrate their children's young lives.

The poem needs its photographs to explain the breathtaking perfection of the Japanese aesthetic as, here, its landscapes connect with the human form to create an idealised unity. When I randomly encountered the mother taking pictures of her beautiful child, I was determined to speak in Japanese so as to give them my own accidental photos, taken at a distance.

I ran the words and their sounds around my head, approached and spoke, and had the most beautiful interaction.

The Photo

The girl was with her mother and her grandmother.
I approached them when I came upon them later
And said I have a photo.

The family was relaxed, the mother
Using her own camera, while the grandmother
Enjoyed the moment.

All eyes of course on the girl,
But they were tender
Without overly coaxing.

My hesitancy disappeared
As I wondered, should I say?
My stranger's *sumi masen,* excuse me, successful.

I held out my upturned palm
My phone showing the photo.
"*Sashin ga arimasu* ... I have a photo."

The mother gasped involuntarily,
The grandmother drew closer, looked,
Then smiled at me broadly.

The little girl ran over
Looked casually at the picture,
Nodded, and was off again.

I set the photo into an email
Handed the phone over
So easily, the photo now with the family.

I had in fact snapped two shots,
I liked the other, the girl leaning to the koi.
I later sent that on as well.

КЧОТО

Japan's Music
2022-11-22/23

In Hagi, Toshiko san and Naoki san's daughter-in-law, Noriko san, had offered to try and arrange a recital of traditional Japanese music for me. I had been saying how much I had wanted to hear and see these musicians and listen to their music, but hadn't come across an opportunity. Perhaps Covid-19 was still limiting performance.

Noriko san's work included arranging for a musician to play this music for just the one person – a personal performance. She offered to find out if this was possible in Kyoto. I had instantly shaken my head and said, "No! I am not that special ..."

I changed my mind sitting on the local bus as it climbed towards Tsuwano. I said to myself that I was in Japan, perhaps for the only time ever. Why was I being so limiting of what was perhaps possible? I contacted Toshiko san to ask Noriko san if it was indeed possible.

The following day, Noriko san connected me to the Kiotto Theatre in Kyoto. A performance had been arranged for me to listen to the koto music of Hirabayashi Ryuten. I would then be staying in Himeji, an easy shinkansen train journey to Kyoto.

The theatre's website (https://kiotto.jp/en/about/) reads,

"Let's visit here again!" is pronounced "Kiotto" in Japanese. "Let's wear a kimono!" is pronounced Kiotto in Japanese. It is a play on words that we use for the name of this establishment and as a way of inviting everyone to enjoy kimono and Japanese culture. This is what Kiotto is built upon.

Kiotto is also a pun on the word "Kyoto" hoping that people who visit Kyoto would enjoy the culture of Kyoto. As a present from Kiotto to all those interested in Kyoto and Japanese culture, we hold Koto experience, Painting experience, and Kimono wearing.

I was hugely humbled to sit, just on my own, in front of the small theatre stage to listen to Hirabayashi Ryuten playing the kokyu and the koto. She is the founder of the Ikuta-Sakamoto style of playing the koto and is also a Master of Azechi kokyu music.

After her performance, I spoke with Hirabayashi san with the help of Ai san from the Kiotto Theatre. On hearing how much I also wanted to listen to the shakuhachi, Hirabayashi san rang her friend and shakuhachi player, Fukai Yuzan. Fukai san agreed to play.

The following day at 1pm, both Hirabayashi Ryuten and Fukai Yuzan played Japan's Music.

We talked after their performances with green tea brought by Ai san who translated once again. My late wife, Aloka, had played the recorder. I shared a picture of her playing her long wooden tenor recorder, a common bond bringing everyone closer.

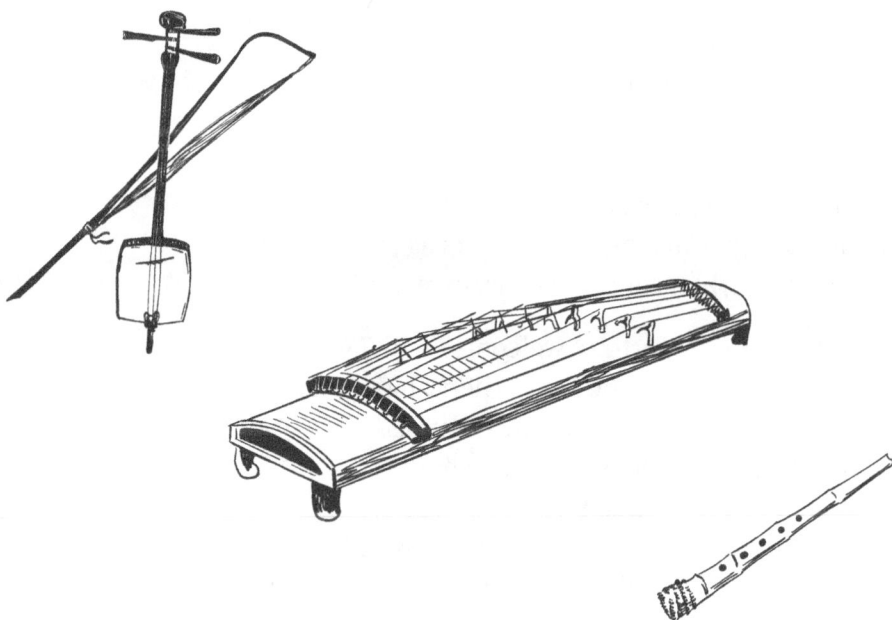

Japan's Music
Hirabayashi Ryuten

The *Kokyu*
Beautiful music, sorrowful and tender.
I am the only member of the audience
As Hirabayashi Ryuten plays the *kokyu* in Kyoto.
It is square like a shamisen, three strings,
Skin stretched across the front and the back,
Played with a long horsehair strung wooden bow.
The *kokyu* is played upright and turned
Each string, one by one, meeting the bow's white hair.
The last song is Hirabayashi Ryuten's own.
She looks to tomorrow, *'Towards the Future'.*

The *Koto*
It is sixty years since Hirabayashi san's hands
First played the 70-inch length
Of the *koto's* paulownia wood.
Its interior hollow, the grain is carved
Like an underground spring, leaving
Its contours on the hidden rocks
To mellow the sounds of the hidden water.
The *koto* though is plucked, sharp aching sounds
Arching through time, over 1000 years as music
Once religious, then adorning court ceremonies.

Hirabayashi san's repertoire welcomed with *'Sakura, Sakura',*
The most celebrated of the *koto's* cherry blossom songs.
Straying then into the formal court sounds,
An old song, pulling me back into an era
I try to imagine, to feel, to forever linger in.
Her voice, her vocal reach powering high and low
Expanding meaning, pulling from and upon my heart.
Her playing keeps me there, her apology
For bringing me out being a modern polyphonic composition.
The *koto* reaches into an orchestra of sound,
I sit in my seat, swaying, journeying into its depths.

Kiotto

The setting is a theatre, *Kiotto*, a wooden building
Looking into a long and ordinary residential street.
I am greeted by Ai san. Ai means 'love' in Japanese.
The nearby station is Saiin,
Where purple trains cross the street
Red warning lights and cyclists temporarily halted.
I had time, so sat and waited nearby, watching,
As young children kicked a ball in a playground.
A girl scudding along on a skateboard!

Fukai Yuzan

Fukai Yuzan is a *shakuhachi* player.
His name means *'The Joy of Playing'*.
Fifty years Yuzan san has played his instrument
Again, I sit alone.
I had returned to the theatre the following day,
Yuzan san and Hirabayashi san had offered to play together.

The *Shakuhachi*

Having played his first song, The Rustling of the Wind,
Yuzan san handed me his *shakuhachi*.
Seven pieces of bamboo,
A forward held flute, blown at the end,
The other end made from the bamboo root.
The player's head rocks back and forth
His neck as a point of balance
Allowing the chin to change position in space
So lowering the pitch of the note,
Adjusting the flute's resonance,
As the wind blows through.

Two songs played, Yuzan san stepped down from the stage.
His mouth hurts, Ai san explained,
It's the *shakuhachi's* nature.
By then I too was overwhelmed, the second tune
Composed in the days succeeding an earthquake.
The rage that this should happen, so many dead,

Softened as the sense in the tune changed
Accepting that this catastrophe too
Is not fixed but obliges us to look to tomorrow.
My body had recalled the images of Hiroshima
The haunting in the notes unforgiving
Of memory and it's fleeting awareness.

The *Koto* and The *Shakuhachi*
Hirabayashi san played once again
The koto lightly releasing the twirls of a songbird.
Her voice too rose and fell, the extraordinary
Possession of this Japanese storytelling.
A music obliging the listener's patience,
No rush to a climax, its story completed
Only once the song was ended.
Taking up his shakuhachi, Yuzan san explained
Their final song was the most celebrated
In the koto's repertoire.

I sat barely moving,
Utterly reluctant that this music should end.
His shakuhachi and the koto of Hirabayashi san
Nonetheless, played for the last time
Easing me through and from these beautiful moments.

Love's Music
The three of us then sat at the table,
Green tea served; I was sincerely honoured.
I showed the first draft of this poem,
Hirabayashi san's picture and the verses already forming
Sufficient to reveal my incomplete intention.
It was exciting as Ai san explained some of what I had written.
She gave me a card with the theatre's email
To send it on once it was finished.
My iPad had stored the picture of my wife, Aloka,
As she played her tenor *recorder* back then in Brittany.
The connection exchanged,
A koto, a kokyu, a shakuhachi, and a *recorder.*

I had been introduced to this perfect good fortune
By Noriko san, when in Hagi she had encouraged
A private recital. I'm not special, I had said.

I am, however, in love with this music.
The beauty of the sounds of these instruments
Has been in my head for decades.
I have not left Japan without hearing them.

Hirabayashi Ryuten and Fukai Yuzan *arigatougozaimasu*

京都

日本の音楽
2022年11月22日から23日

萩で、トシコさんとナオキさんの息子の嫁のノリコさんが、私のために邦楽のリサイタルを開こうとしてくれました。私が邦楽の演奏をぜひこの目で見て、聞きたいと言ったからです。でもその機会はありませんでした。コロナのせいで、まだ演奏活動に制限があったのでしょう。

ノリコさんは、音楽家の演奏をアレンジするのが仕事で、たったひとりの観客のための演奏も手配します。京都で可能かどうか調べてくれるとのことですが、私は首を振りました。「とんでもない！ 私はそんな特別な人間ではありませんよ……」

でも津和野に向かうバスの中で、私は気持ちを変えました。日本を訪れるのは、たった1度きりかもしれない。なぜできることを制限してしまうのか？ 私はトシコさんに連絡して、ノリコさんに可能かどうか聞いてもらいました。

翌日ノリコさんが、京都の京町家Kiotto（きおっと）を紹介してくれました。平林龍典さんの琴の演奏を聞く手配をしてくれたのです。私は姫路泊の予定の日ですが、京都まで新幹線で簡単に行くことができました。

ウェブサイトにはこのように書かれています。(https://kiotto.jp/about/)

「『また来おっと！』と思っていただけるような、ワクワクする空間に。そして『きもの着おっと！』と気軽にきものや和文化を楽しんでいただけるようなお店に。という思いを込めて、『きおっと』は生まれました。

Kiottoは "Kioto＝京都" との掛け言葉でもあり、京都に観光に来られた方々に京都の文化をゆっくり五感で感じ、楽しんでいただきたい。その第一歩として三つの体験（琴・手描き・きもの着付け）をご用意しました。」

小さな舞台での前にたった1人で座り、平林龍典さんの胡弓と琴の演奏を聴くなんて、とても恐縮しました。彼女は生田流阪本派代表で、畦地胡弓音楽院師範なのです。

演奏後、Kiottoの愛さんの助けで、平林さんとお話ししました。私がぜひ尺八を聞きたいと言うと、平林さんが友人の尺八奏者である深井遊山さんに電話をし、演奏に応じてくださったのです。

翌日午後1時に、平林龍典さんと深井遊山さんが邦楽を演奏してくださいました。

演奏後に、愛さんが出してくれた緑茶を飲みながら、また通訳を介して話をしました。私の亡き妻アローカは、リコーダーを演奏しました。妻が長い木製のテナー・リコーダーを演奏している写真を見せると、絆が深まりました。

日本の音楽

平林龍典
胡弓
美しい音楽、哀しくやさしく
観客は私だけ
平林龍典が京都で胡弓を奏でる
三味線のように四角く、3本の弦
前面と裏面は革張り
長い馬毛を張った木製の弓で奏でる
胡弓をまっすぐに立てて、角度を変えながら
弦が1本ずつ、弓の白い毛に出会う
最後は平林龍典の曲
明日を見据え「未来へ」を演奏

琴
60年前に初めて、平林さんの手が
180センチ近い琴に触れた
桐でできた琴
中は空洞で、木目があり
まるで地下の泉のように
隠れた岩の表面を伝わって
奥深い水の音を和らげる
琴を爪引くと、鋭い心疼く音
千年以上の時をつなぐ
宗教や宮廷行事を彩った音

最初に演奏したのは「さくら さくら」
桜の花を唄う、最も有名な琴の曲
そして宮中の音へ
私も昔の時代へと遡り

想像し、感じ、永遠に心さまよう
声は、高く低くも力強く歌う
私の心を揺さぶって、思いが広がってゆく
古き時代に引き込まれ
現代の多声音楽から離れてゆく
琴が音色のオーケストラとなり
私は座ったまま、体を揺らし、深みへと旅してゆく

きおっと

木造のKiottoの舞台は
普通の住宅街の道沿いにある
"愛"さんに迎えられる
最寄駅は西院
紫色の電車が通りを横切る
赤い警告灯で自転車が一旦止まる
時間はあるので、近くに座って見ていた
小さな子供たちが、公園でボールを蹴る
少女がスケートボードで滑走していく！

深井遊山

深井遊山は尺八奏者
"遊びを楽しむ"と言う名前
尺八を演奏して50年
また私はひとりで聞いた
翌日もまた演奏の場に戻り
遊山さんと平林さんが合奏してくれた

尺八

最初の曲「The Rustling of the Wind」を
弾いた後に
遊山さんは私に尺八を渡す
竹の7つの節
前に持って、端に息を吹き込む
先は竹の根でできている
奏者は頭を前後へ揺らし
首でバランスをとり
顎の位置を変える

音を低くし
笛の共鳴を調整し
風を吹き込むように

2曲演奏した後、遊山さんは舞台をおりた
口が痛むからと、愛さんが説明する
それが尺八
2曲目には私も圧倒された
地震直後に作られた曲
なぜこんなことが起きたのか
こんなに人が亡くなったのか
怒りから、やがて調べが和らぐ
災害を受け止め
未来へと向かうしかない
私の体は、広島を思い出す
情け容赦ない音色につきまとう
記憶と覚醒

琴と尺八
また平林さんが演奏する
琴の音が、鳥の歌声を解き放つ
声も高くなり、低くなり
日本の語り部の見事な力
聞き手の忍耐力を試すように
クライマックスを急がず
曲が終わるまで物語は続く
尺八を手に、遊山さんが説明する
最後の曲は琴の楽曲の中で
最も有名なものだと

私は身じろぎもせず
音楽が終わらないで欲しいと思う
遊山さんの尺八と平林さんの琴
でも最後の曲の
美しい時間に身を委ねる

愛の音楽

3人で卓を囲み
緑茶をいただく光栄に預かる
この詩の下書きを見せる
平林さんの写真と
出来かけの詩で
未完成ながら伝わる
一部を愛さんが説明してくれて嬉しい
彼女の名刺にメールアドレスがある
書き上げたら、送ろう
私のiPadには、妻のアローカの写真
ブルターニュでテナー・リコーダーを演奏した時の写真だ
絆が生まれる
琴、胡弓、尺八、そしてリコーダー

この幸運な巡り合いは
萩のノリコさんのおかげだ
プライベート・リサイタルなんて私には勿体ないと思った

でも、私は邦楽が好きで
楽器の音色の美しさは
何十年も頭にあった
日本を去る前に聞かなくてはならない

平林龍典さん、深井遊山さん
アリガトウゴザイマス

HIMEJI IZAKAYA

2022-11-22/23

In Japan, from the day I arrived until the morning I left, I moved from one cocoon of unconditioned hospitality to another. A ramen izakaya in Himeji was one of those cocoons. An izakaya is a bar and diner – this one in Himeji served ramen, a noodle dish served in a broth, and was called Ramen Izakaya.

The Ramen Izakaya was a minute's step from the flat above the kimono shop where I was staying. I went there on two nights, the second being the evening of my return from Kyoto, when I had listened to Hirabayashi Ryuten and Fukai Yuzan's music. Hirabayashi Ryuten had given me a CD of her music – and signed it. I took it with me to the izakaya, hoping that I may have a chance to listen to it there.

So, I came into the izakaya that evening still enraptured by the music earlier that day. The evening unfolded as if a film or theatre director had its hand as the owner, Koba san, welcomed me and allowed us both to open into some of our stories as I watched him prepare my ramen meal. As we did, his jazz radio and my Japanese music played us through the evening.

I also ate Koba san's delicious *gyoza* on both evenings – crispy pan-fried dumplings, golden on the bottom and juicy on the inside.

The following day, I had asked the owner of the kimono shop if I could buy some kimono cloth, to take back to my daughters. Instead, she gave me five Japanese styled teddy bears, four of them made using kimono material. Her flat was filled with old furnishings, paintings, posters, art, and curiosity objects. The bears had been sitting variously around the rooms. She said it was time they went on their way!

This story is not in the poem – it should have one of its own:
本当にごめんなさい! *hontōni gomen nasai* ! I'm truly sorry!

Koba san's ramen izakaya is at: *Ramen Izakaya, 59 Gofukumachi, Himeji 670-0923, Hyogo Prefecture*

The Ramen Izakaya

Hardly 100 yards from the kimono shop,
A red banner at its door, is the ramen izakaya.
I am welcomed in, the only customer.
A little later joined by one more,
He though, ate and was soon gone.
The owner ushered me to the far end of the bar,
Being the most hospitable, the furthest from the door.
He stood there at the far end when not cooking
Intent on engaging, ensuring conversation.

The menu was of course dishes of ramen,
I had the pork with a soft-boiled egg alongside.
First of all, though, I asked for the gyoza.
The following night I went back,
Asked for the gyoza again, they were so delicious.
Koba san, the jazz loving owner, was pleased to know,
He not only cooks them, it's also he who makes them.

The izakaya was warm, it took seconds only
To feel at home. Ease was instant, everything
Personally in place, even the T-shirts Koba san wore
Were his own designs, humorously printing
The front jacket cover of jazz albums.
The music was live streamed from New York.
It felt as if I could come in here every night.

I hadn't seen ramen cooked before, it was an art.
The stove had its hotplates, on one of those
A heavy frying pan prepared the gyoza.
When the time was felt right to check,
Koba san lifted a little and looked at the undersides.
A colour just gone past caramelised brown
They were ready and plated, just them with soya.
My mouth is remembering the soft texture
The lightest of bites, the spiced taste.

There was a precise order to the cooking.
A sunken vat of boiling water was the centre of the stove,
Steam pouring out when the lid was lifted for the ramen.
The variation to the dish, the second night was with tofu,
That was cooked to the right, the pan to the left
Was for the gyoza only, scraped scrupulously clean
After each use, set aside carefully.
Koba san was a chef, he wasn't preparing a ready meal.
I looked on fascinated as each element to a simple dish
Was pulled together with practiced dexterity.

Even removing the ramen from the packet
Was done with finesse.
The noodles were expertly thrown into the vat.
The technique ensuring they remained separate
On contact with the water, I presumed.
A couple of lifts with a long handled flat sieve
The noodles then left lidded till finished.
The temperature was controlled by a little cold water
A tap placed right above the pot, turned on briefly
At the point of the ramen being ready.
A swift check of the pan to the right
Koba swept out the noodles, threw them in the air
To get rid of excess water, the same flat sieve.

The broth with the ramen he created by adding water
To the pan with the chosen ingredients
Not all at once but measured by sense then reduced.
Spices and sauces differentiating one from the other.
The soft tofu added with just enough time to warm through.
I enjoyed both to the last drop and to the last noodle.

Koba had enough words of English to allow
Us both to give a little away of the other.
He wore a blue scarf wrapped tightly round his head
Knotted at the back, I want to say Japanese style.
Our taste in modern jazz was exactly shared

Meaning the names of the greats were said with affection.
Inhibition diminished, he pulled the curtain to the back aside
Said this is my hobby, a sound system fitted to the ceiling!
I hadn't realised that it was the quality of his system
That was making the music so enjoyable. I do now.

Inevitably we strayed, being two nights long, to why my journey.
He said he was in his 50s and hadn't travelled,
But he said his wife did, all over the world. They had two children.
He learned to say 'cheers' in Scots Gaelic ... slainte!
On the bar shelf were a few notes in foreign currency.
There wasn't one in sterling, so now there is my £10 note.
A farewell to Queen Elizabeth II acknowledged,
Her portrait now commemorated in a Himeji izakaya.
There were three people there when I arrived the second night.
Two Japanese women and an American man from Portland.
Enviably, he was speaking Japanese fluently.
He had worked in Japan, met his partner,
Now living in the States, they had returned for a visit.
I briefly enjoyed the encounter as they left soon after.

I had brought with me the CD from Kyoto.
I asked if I could hear it played in Japan.
For the next hour we listened, volume set to a good level.
The *koto*, the *kokyu*, the *shakuhachi*,
Those same wondrous musicians
I had heard play just a few hours earlier.
Koba carefully removed the notes from the case
Read them, explaining each of the songs as they came.
We listened, a different mood from the jazz,
Not so carefree, more withdrawn, a wanderer's storytelling.

Koba reached over the counter and shook my hand when I left.

姫路　居酒屋

2022年11月22日から23日

　日本では、到着した日から帰国する朝まで、次から次へと無条件のもてなしの繭に包まれていました。姫路のラーメン居酒屋も、その繭の1つでした。

　その店は、私が滞在していた呉服屋の2階の部屋から徒歩1分でした。2回そこで食事しましたが、2晩目は京都で平林龍典さんと深井遊山さんの演奏を聞いた後でした。平林龍典さんは自分のサイン入りのCDをくださったので、それを聞けたらいいなと思って、持っていきました。

　だから、店に着いた時の私は、聴いたばかりの邦楽で頭がいっぱいでした。でもその晩は、映画か演劇の監督が演出したような展開となりました。迎えてくれたオーナーのコバさんと、お互いの身の上話をしながら、私はラーメンを準備する様子を見ていました。その背後では、ラジオからのジャズや、私の邦楽が流れました。

　2晩続けて、コバさんの美味しい餃子を食べました。香ばしくカリッと焼いた餃子は、外は黄金色で、中はジューシーでした。

　翌日、呉服屋のオーナーに、娘たちのために着物の生地を買いたいと相談しました。すると、その代わりに、彼女は日本風のテディベアを5つくれました。そのうち4つは着物の生地で作られていました。家は古家具やポスター、絵画や面白いもので溢れていて、部屋のあちこちにテディベアが座っていました。彼女はそろそろ彼らも我が道をゆく頃だと言うのです！

　この物語は詩に書いていません。書けばよかった。

　ホントニゴメンナサイ

　Koba & More (コバモア)
　郵便番号670-0923 兵庫県姫路呉服町59

ラーメン居酒屋

呉服屋から100メートルほど
赤いのぼりが立っている
迎えられた客は私だけ
後になって、もう1人いたが
食べるとすぐに出て行った
オーナーは私を奥に座らせる
入口から遠く、居心地がいい
調理していない時はオーナーが来て
おしゃべりに夢中になる

メニューは各種ラーメン
豚肉と半熟卵を選ぶ
でもまずは餃子
あまりに美味しかったので
翌晩戻って、また餃子を注文した
ジャズ愛好家のコバさんは喜んでくれた
餃子は焼くだけでなく、自家製だ

店は暖かく居心地がよく
すぐにくつろいだ
すべて個性にあふれ、コバさんが着ているTシャツも
自らのユーモラスなデザインで
ジャズ・アルバムのジャケットのプリント
音楽はニューヨークからのライブ配信
毎晩でも通いたくなる

初めて見た芸術的なラーメン作り
コンロの上には
重いフライパンで餃子を焼いている
頃合いをみて
コバさんは少し餃子を持ち上げて見る
黄金色が少し濃くなったら出来上がり
皿に盛り、醤油だけ添えて
その柔らかい食感が忘れられない
口当たりは軽く、スパイスが効いている

調理には厳密な段取りがある
コンロの中央に煮えたぎるお湯
蓋を開けると湯気が溢れ出る
2晩目は少し変えて豆腐を注文
右には鍋を、左にはフライパン
餃子専用のフライパンは、きちんとこそげ落とし
使い終わるたび、丁寧に傍に置く
コバさんは料理人、市販品は使わない
私が興味津々に見ている前で
材料を1つ1つ
熟練した腕でまとめ上げる

麺を袋から出す時さえも
見事な手際のよさ
お湯の中に投げ込まれた麺は
湯の中でもくっつかない
それも巧みな技なのか
長い柄のついた平らなザルを数回揺すり
茹であがるまで蓋
温度調整は少しの冷水で
鍋の真上の蛇口をほんの少し回す
ラーメンの出来上がり
右の鍋を確認し
麺を取り出し、宙に投げ
同じザルで水を切る

自家製のラーメンの汁は
様々な材料に湯を加えたもの
秤は使わず、感覚で調節する
調味料やソースはそれぞれ違う
柔らかい豆腐は温めるだけ
汁の最後の一滴、麺の最後の一本まで、じっくり味わった

コバさんは多少英語がわかるので
話をするには十分だった
頭に青いスカーフをしっかり巻いて
後ろで結ぶのは、日本風か
モダン・ジャズの好みはぴったり
名演奏家の名を愛情込めて語り合う
遠慮は消え、彼が後ろのカーテンを開けると
趣味の音響システムが天井まで!
そこまで高品質だったとは
だから音楽が楽しめたのだと、やっとわかる

2晩を過ごせば、おのずと私の旅の理由も語る
彼は50代だが、旅行はしない
妻は世界中を旅し、子供は2人
彼はスコットランドのゲール語で乾杯と言える。スラーンチェ!
バーの棚には数枚の外貨の紙幣
ポンド紙幣は見当たらないので、私の10ポンド紙幣を加えた
エリザベス2世を追悼し
姫路の店に肖像を残す
2晩目には先客が3人
2人の日本人女性と、ポートランド出身のアメリカ人男性
羨ましくも彼は日本語を流暢に話す
日本で仕事をし、伴侶に出会い
今はアメリカで暮らすが、里帰りしていた
短い出会いを楽しんだが、彼らはすぐに出て行った

京都からCDを持ってきていた
日本で聞きたいと頼み
それから1時間鑑賞し、音量もちょうどいい
琴、胡弓、尺八
驚くべき音楽家たち
数時間前に生演奏を聞いたばかり
コバさんはケースから丁寧に冊子をとり
それぞれの曲の解説を読んでくれた
ジャズとは違うムード
気楽ではなく、より内省的な、放浪者の物語

私の去り際に、コバさんがカウンターから手を伸ばし、握手を交わす

TOKYO

A Night and A Day in Tokyo
2022-11-24/25

I had arrived in Japan with a plan. The plan had been a balance between linking dates to places and having time in those places to wander and walk. As well as limiting distance to the central island of Honshu, the plan had left out visiting the big cities of Tokyo and Osaka. I hadn't wanted the craze of the noise, the crush, the lights, the biggest museums …

And each day, the plan had revealed itself perfectly.

Tokyo was therefore my departure point, to briefly visit and leave. Briefly, though, meant two nights in the Asakusa district. Asakusa is the older Tokyo, a short trip from the main station to the Tawaramachi metro station and my hotel – and not far, a walking distance, from the National Museum. I was content with two whole days to cross the famous and world's busiest Shibuya giant pedestrian crossing and generally to absorb being in Tokyo.

One of the days in Tokyo was also my birthday and I had bought a ticket to go to a jazz club on the birthday evening!

It may be that I brought my apprehension with me as my train arrived in the outskirts of the metropolis. It was night, so dark, and the press of the never ending landscape of tall buildings, commerce, and industry seemed in blunt and unpleasant contrast to the beauty I had been wrapped in during the previous four weeks.

My apprehension was not unfounded, transgressing even within the objects in the National Museum. At the same time, the museum's kimonos and landscape paintings were wondrous, leaving me in stilled contemplation.

And of course, there was the individual encounter in a tiny coffee shop, where the same gentle and interested acceptance was given by the young barista.

A Night and A Day in Tokyo

The Shinkansen enters the vastness that is Tokyo.
In the darkness of this evening, I feel discomfort.
I don't want to get off, already claustrophobic.
I take the wrong exit, into a square of giant buildings.
Finding the Metro, I make my way to Tawaramachi.

Unsettled and unwilling to read or begin a poem
I decide to walk out, find an ATM.
The area is Asakusa, a nightlife bright, noisy, bustling.
I wander through the side streets
A red light district. A young woman
Looking cold and wearing a coat
Stands at a bar door, calling out to passers-by.
A sign advertises *sweet girls inside.*
Following another corner, I come face to face
With the illuminated street down to the Sensoji Temple.
It's Tokyo's biggest, also a nighttime attraction.

In the morning I go back to Sensoji for another look.
The tourists are voracious, louder, the small stalls
Selling wishes and bracelets, crushed one upon the other.
A prayer bead necklace was on my mind,
I look at the prices, I turn away dispirited.
Before leaving, I climb the steps to light a candle,
It is a temple, and I have come inside.

The morning side streets are empty of the night.
It's gone 10 and shops remain closed, or just opening.
I stay away from the main roads, the street pattern a grid
So once understood, easy to wander to the museum.
I walk past two shops, each next door, selling only knives.
Small restaurants are abundant, lots of chefs.
Work is going on all around, road drills and deliveries,
But I'm glad of the otherwise silence.

Up ahead, perched on a corner, is a tiny coffee shop.
I know as it says *Ristretto* above the door.
I'm not sure if it's open, others weren't.
I go in, see three stools, ask for a cappuccino.
It's not chic, but it is city urban, the barista a young woman
Owning a few words of English to match my Japanese.
I ask if she has drawn the notebook sized manga
Three of which are for sale on the shelf where I sit.
She says no, they are by her friend, only a few printed.
I buy two, they are real, really made in Tokyo!
I walk past much later and take a photo.

Next stop The National Museum. I join the ticket queue.
The standing exhibition is not in demand,
Of the woodblock prints on display, two were by Hiroshige,
Two by Hokusai, including one of his scenes of Mt Fuji.
I was pleased, the other prints raising questions.
Many of them scenes of kabuki actors playing women.
More were scenes of pleasure houses and courtesans
Exquisitely dressed and accomplished in music,
Images made by men for men.
A long hand-painted scroll reveals their story,
The same business as the night before.
The representations alluring and fantasised
Encouraging visitors through the same red-light gates.

The kimonos presented themselves in a cabinet of beauty,
The intricacies of the patterns, the needlework, and the dyes
The uninhibited intention of the wearer
To be fashionable and to dare.
Six screens range across the four seasons
Each seven feet tall, five feet wide and 700 years old.
A grey monochromatic ink landscape startlingly reveals
Spring, summer, autumn, and winter, connected
As pine trees, fledgling ducks, cranes, clouds,
Flowers in bloom, and birds in flight.
Sits me still for an hour, the hand of
Kano Motonobu, once serving a samurai lord.

TOKYO - THE PIT INN
IN SHINJUKU.

2022-11-26

The 26th of November, my birthday. I was happy to be in Japan, backpacking. I was happy to celebrate being here and to do so in a Jazz Club in Tokyo, The Pit Inn. My plan for visiting Japan had had a very simple perspective – to have everything around me happen freely and for it to do so without my taking a scalpel to what was underneath.

I was a tourist, on his own, in a personal space. I was not looking at the underlying harms which betray the superficial harmony of any society.

And so, to a small celebration; a coffee and cake in the bookshop area of a classic department store by the Shibuya crossing, a visit to a museum, a meal in the evening in the bustling nighttime Shinjuku area before heading to a jazz club.

Tokyo, The Pit Inn, in Shinjuku.

I had a couple of hours to spare before 7pm
The email had said that's when
I had to collect my ticket for the jazz club.
I was for sure at the top of the list. (I was!)
First in, first to the choice of seats.
I sat three rows from the front, no tables,
The room small, just customers, a bar, and a stage.

The Italian restaurant suited my mood,
Coming across it in the busy Shinjuku Street
A surprise. Sometime later, some wine, Frascati Superiore,
And I was ready to face the music ...

The day had gone according to plan,
A visit to the museum, Chinese art back to 1700 BC.
I admired the beautiful sculptured Buddhas,
The rare bronzes, and the early porcelain.
The exhibition however drawing me in, was
The mounting of those astonishing Japanese screens
Depicting the seasons, the rice being cultivated,
Birds and flowers, pine trees, and fishermen.
I said all this yesterday, I remain as enraptured.

At the museum's shop
A small piece of gold purchased ...
As a pin for my jacket,
1951 the year of the rabbit
Today being my birthday.

The Nezu museum also has a garden,
More densely designed than in Kyoto and Himeji.
The rain had torrented, stopping only an hour previously,
It was the smell of the earth which left its mark
As I walked down paths, around and up again.
The ceremonial tearoom was closed to a private event
A glimpse of traditional wear, women and men.

The museum's street was lined with luxury,
The fashionable Ayoma district, iconic stores,
Their European names – Stella McCartney among them.

The Prada store architecture briefly caught my eye
Rising as it did, an imposing glass geometrical structure,
"To reshape both the concept and function
Of shopping, pleasure and communication,
To encourage the meshing of consumption and culture."

I read those words on an online commentary.
The jazz was ok ... I wish I could say more.
So standard, even Summertime given a go.
I was disappointed, the band's leader a percussionist,
His first solo half an hour before he introduced
The rest of the band ... tenor sax ... piano ... double bass.
The band more accompanists than their own players
The pianist effortless and beautifully fluent,
When sometimes, his own hands let loose.

Next to me were two men, one from New Zealand,
He was married to a teacher and had two children,
The teenage girl a bit of a horror he said.
He took lots of photographs.
The American was softer. Though not saying why
He was very thin, an illness. I mentioned my birthday
He said it would be great if he were to live as long as 71.

I loved it though, so I'll say it again ...
On my 71st birthday, I was in a jazz club
In Tokyo, The Pit Inn, in Shinjuku.

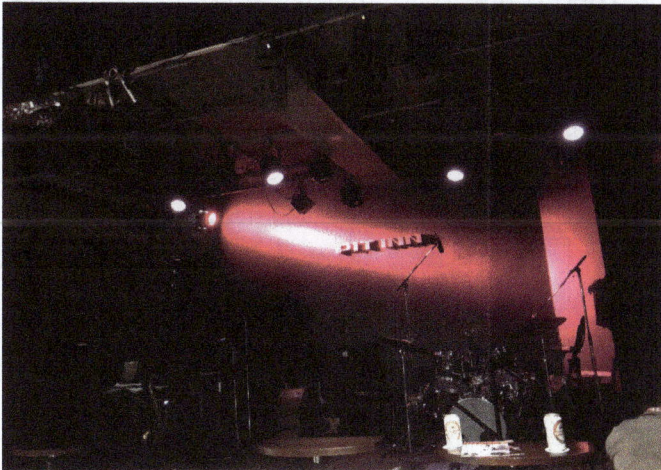

TOKYO - ARIGATOUGOZAIMASU

2022-11-27/28

ありがとうございます This means thank you.

This last poem in Japan was written on the last evening as I spoiled myself by staying at a hotel inside the airport!

There was to be no last moment disappointment though, as I floated into and out of the hotel onto my plane – Japanese courtesy and consideration continuous.

I had travelled there on the Tokyo underground – via two of its enormous stations – then by local overland train crammed with stressed passengers also on their way to the airport. That though was intentional as I had wanted to breathe in Japan's last moments for as long as I could.

A surprisingly fine restaurant and fine meal was another last gift. This was the hotel's own, very smooth, allowing me to adjust with easy last thoughts and just the right flavours, as I began my detachment from Japan. A gentle bookending was the glass of Hibiki whisky. I had only recently come across Hibiki and that was in a newly opened little wine bar near my own home – it was touching to have the geographies connected.

As well, on the last full day, I had sat in a grand Tokyo theatre listening to a concert of classical music – a last minute ticket success. A holiday concert, it had included a song about a red dragonfly, *akatombo*. This provided more fond sentiment, connecting an earlier visit to my daughter in Singapore and to my teacher of Japanese, Lisa sensei.

This poem is the fullest possible thank you to the entirety of my time in Japan. *Arigatougozaimasu.*

Miso soup is a traditional Japanese soup
sashimi is raw fish eaten with soy sauce and wasabi paste
yakitori is a type of skewered chicken
eki is the Japanese word for station

ありがとうございます

Arigatougozaimasu.
Thank you.

I had come down to the bar from the table
Where I had had my last meal in Japan.
Miso soup, sashimi, posed perfectly on a green mint leaf.
Various small, perfectly cut pieces of pickled vegetable,
A saucer of soya and two kinds of wasabi, a bowl of rice.
All of these in their own delicate dish,
The yakitori on its sticks, that too invitingly glazed.

I savoured the slow pace of the chopsticks.
A glass of Japanese whisky to see the evening out.
Hibiki, Harmony blend.
First found in the town where I live,
In the Little Wine Bar in Walton.

I'm in Terminal 3, Tokyo's Haneda Airport.
It's once in a lifetime, so I booked the hotel,
The Royal Park where its front door
Walks you straight into the terminal and onto the plane.
Spoiled, I know, and also quite delicious!

This morning I had left Tokyo's Tawaramchi eki,
Taken my bags with me and left them in a locker
At Shinjuku eki. The station is huge!
Later I found myself changing lines in Shinagawa.
Whole worlds exist in these stations!
The blogs all said catch the airport coach
Perhaps I should have followed their advice
But I wanted to enjoy every last minute of Japan.

Not quite being lost in various enormous stations,
Teeming with people and just being with them,
Was how I wanted to remember.

Earlier this year in February and March,
I had stood and watched a red dragonfly.
It was flitting around the edge of a pond
At home in Singapore's Botanic Garden.
Its flight and red colour seemed full of wonder,
I felt its good fortune and stood a long time watching.
Later, I spoke with Lisa sensei in our Japanese lesson.
She gave me the word for a red dragonfly,
'Akatombo' ...

In Japan, red dragonflies are held sacred,
Offering a symbol of courage, strength, and happiness.
A song 'Akatombo', from an early 20th century poem,
Is celebrated. An infant observing the dragonfly
Landing on his sister's shoulder, soon to be married and gone.
Lisa sensei sent me a link and so I had become familiar with its tune.

The jazz night was Saturday, I was leaving on the Monday.
Rather late, I looked for a concert on the Sunday.

The Tokyo Philharmonic Orchestra
Had its Holiday Afternoon Concert, The 95th!
And there on the programme was the song *'Akatombo'*.
There was just the one seat left in the stalls, Row 24, Seat 4.
Goodness, this good fortune. A previous life perhaps rewarded.
Dvorak's music was good natured, no saddening drama departure!
The soprano, Maki Mori, joining for her suite of songs,
One of those, *'Akatombo'*.

So here I am with a coffee in the morning
Said *Ohayogozaimasu*, good morning, in the café.
Counted out the exact change, 583 yen ... was pleased.
Said my very last thank you to Japan.
Head bowed,

Arigatougozaimasu.
ありがとうございます

The scene below is of The Sea of Japan seen from Hagi.

A JAPAN POSTSCRIPT

Thank You

For the temple bell charm
To grasp in my hand
When uncertain.

.

.

.

My legs,
My back that carried my bag,
I honour them.

.

.

.

My clothes,
A walker's warm vest
Seamless socks
And so on

.

.

.

The poems I wrote
Their company
At night
And in the morning
When alone.

.

.

.

A teacher,
Lisa Omura
A poet,
Kaneko Misuzu

The electronics
Where I placed my foot
With words translated

.
.
.

The words
Sumimasen
Onegaishimasu
Arigatougozaimasu

.
.
.

Just with these three words
And a respectful smile,
All of Japan
Is yours to travel

.
.
.

Thank you.

日本　あとがき

ありがとう

寺の鐘のお守り
不安な時に
手で握る

脚たちよ
荷を担いだ背中よ
おかげさま

我が服よ
ウォーキング用の暖かなベストや
シームレスな靴下たち
いろいろに

自作の詩
旅の道づれ
日暮れにも
朝になっても
ひとりの時も

先生たち
オオムラ・リサと
詩人
金子みすゞ

電子機器
叩けば
翻訳してくれる

言葉たち
スミマセン
オネガイシマス
アリガトウゴザイマス

この3つのフレーズと
相手を敬う笑顔があれば
日本のどこを旅しても
きっと大丈夫

ありがとう

www.ingramcontent.com/pod-product-compliance
Lightning Source LLC
Chambersburg PA
CBHW062104080426
42734CB00012B/2747